NGOs in SAARC Countries

NGOs *in* SAARC Countries

Ravi Ranjan

Prashant Publishing House
DELHI - 110094 (INDIA)

PRASHANT PUBLISHING HOUSE
C-34, 28 Foota Road, Gali No. 3
West Karawal Nagar, Delhi-110094
Phone : 9810396373, 22963970

NGOs in SAARC Countries

First Published : 2009

ISBN : 978-81-908282-3-9

PRINTED IN INDIA

Published by Mr. R. K. Jha M/s. Prashant Publishing House, Delhi and Printed at H.S. Offset Press, Delhi.

PREFACE

The South Asian people share many socio-economic and political problems, such as poverty, illiteracy, unemployment, unequal treatment of women, violence against women, pollution, exploitation of child labor, and religious fundamentalism. Human rights organizations in South Asia have recently taken steps to cooperate in addressing their common problems. Almost all South Asian countries have laws that do not respect essential notions of due process, often resulting in arbitrary arrests, assault, and killing of innocent people by government officials. For instance, freedom of movement between countries is highly restricted. India and Pakistan often deny visas to their citizens, and even when granted, these governments require travelers to report daily to police stations in the town they are visiting.

More than two million Nepalese women are working as prostitutes in Indian brothels, where approximately 20% are girls below 16 years of age. Women and children are bought and sold into prostitution. The Nepalese- speaking people of Bhutan are suffering under the monarchy's state policy of ethnic cleansing, whereby they are compelled to leave Bhutan and take shelter in countries such as India and Nepal. The Sinhalese-controlled government of Sri Lanka is struggling to control a separatist movement, led by the Tamil minority, and disappearances, bombing in public areas, and random death are common. The Bangladeshi government continues to use force to suppress the armed resistance of indigenous people who are seeking to become politically independent, and the crops and houses of innocent people are being destroyed in the process.

— *Author*

CONTENTS

1

IMPLICATIONS FOR NGO MANAGEMENT

The concept of 'community-based action' is ubiquitous in the current development policy discourse amongst NGOs. This paper presents a critical look at the management issues involved in implementing community-based action. It is shown that community-based action can be implemented by NGOs in two ways; NGOs can either link with pre-existing community-based organisations (CBOs) or can create new community-based organisations. Each involves distinct management challenges. A consideration of these challenges with use of examples, mainly from Uganda, suggests that the way that the concept of community is used in development discourse often ignores the realities of community dynamics. The paper suggests ways in which NGOs can begin to develop a more relevant concept of community with which to work.

INTRODUCTION

Much of the literature which focuses on the role of non-governmental organisations (NGOs) in development has been characterised by interest in policy issues for NGO relations with states, donors and communities (Lewis 1998: 3). In comparison literature that takes as its theme NGO management is small, if growing. The tendency to privilege issues of policy over issues of management in the NGO development discourse is striking in the light of the practical and organisational nature of the work of NGOs.

There are two reasons why there should be greater attention given to issues of NGO management. First, NGOs concerned with development face the management of a complex and diverse range of issues. NGOs face internal management issues, for example questions of strategic planning, budgeting, staffing, the governing structure of the organisation, growth and change within the organisation. NGOs also face the management of external relationships; relations with government, the private sector, other NGOs and with their target communities. All of these come to bear on the possibility of NGOs managing development. The effectiveness of NGOs as actors in development and change depends on successful engagement with both internal and external management questions and also on the successful articulation between issues of internal and external management (De Graaf 1987: 297). Second, the consideration of NGO management issues is important because turning policy into effective action requires effective management. A critical realisation that the implementation of policy directives is a practical rather than ideological process is often missing in NGO literature. The underlying theme of this paper is that NGOs who work in development can reap benefits by considering the practical and managerial implications for the implementation of policy ideas.

'Community-based action' is a policy idea that pervades the contemporary NGO development discourse. It is part of a strategic shift that NGOs have made in their relationship with the people that they work with and for, their beneficiaries. Fowler (1997: 221) has described this strategic shift as one in which NGOs move from roles of welfare and delivery to roles of strengthening people's organisations and movements.3 The shift has occurred in tandem with an overall recognition of the importance of alternative, grassroots approaches to development processes (Craig & Mayo 1995: 1).

A whole set of now commonly used ideas and terms have accompanied this strategic shift. One of the most ubiquitous concepts advocated in the NGO development discourse is for the 'participation' of beneficiaries in development processes. Buijs (quoted in Carroll 1992: 78) defines people's participation as ... a process of change in which members of the project group by common effort gain an increasing influence in the decision making of their organisation The reasoning is that participation encourages the formulation of development strategies that are increasingly sustainable, people centered and just. Hand in hand with the concept of participation has been the idea of 'empowerment'. Empowerment of beneficiaries has become a standard cited aim of NGOs involved in development work. The idea here is that the relationship between NGOs and their beneficiaries acts as a catalyst to a process in which target communities develop greater awareness and control over the power structures that determine their lives. Likewise the strategic shift made by NGOs in the relationship with their beneficiaries has entailed promotion of the concept of 'social capital' for NGOs to foster and use in development and change amongst the people with whom they work. Social capital has been defined as: ... features of social organisation, such as trust, norms and networks that can improve the efficiency of society by facilitating coordinating actions. (Putnam 1993: 167)

Recognition of the importance of social capital is thus recognition of indigenous resources that might be consolidated for development. Like the concepts of participation and empowerment, the notion of social capital has gained ground in the climate of decentralisation in development thinking and for NGOs involved in development

(Harriss 1997: 928). There are both practical and ideological incentives for such decentralisation. On a practical level development action driven by concepts such as participation, empowerment and the consolidating of social capital promises to reach the poorest in efficient and cost effective ways (Mayo & Craig 1995: 2). On an ideological level it promises a change in the balance of power within development processes, one in which beneficiaries move from receivers to contributors. However, despite the advantages cited and the prevalence of ideas that stress the importance of grassroots development in all range of NGOs and development agencies, there is much rhetoric and little exactitude about the concepts involved.

The bundle of ideas about the 'right' relationship between NGOs and their beneficiaries comes to bear on the advocacy of community-based action. Here community is taken as the proper and most effective site in which NGOs can work as an agent of change whilst incorporating ideals of participation, social capital and empowerment. This paper will consider the translation of 'community-based action' from a concept implied in NGO rhetoric to its practical manifestation in NGO development work. It will be shown that whilst the translation of community-based action into practice has many advantages in the creation of participatory, empowering development, it is not as smooth and unproblematic as might be suggested by the prevalence of the use of the concept in the NGO development discourse. There will be consideration of the strengths and weaknesses of community-based action drawn from case studies and suggestions as to how these might have implications for NGO management.

COMMUNITY-BASED ACTION

The 'community-based action' approach can be found in NGO policy in multiple and diverse areas of development.

Thus a manual on NGO intervention in the area of psychological trauma amongst children after war experiences stresses: There is an absolute necessity of turning to communities, families and children themselves as proactive participants in the analysis of their own situation and opportunities, in assessing their needs and resources and designing and carrying out solutions, trusting local and traditional methods. (Reichenberg & Friedman 1995: 321 for UNICEF) Such sentiments credit people with the ability, even in the most extreme circumstances, to engage with the issues that face them. It is an important corrective to seeing people as passive victims of circumstances, an image which is in danger of being promoted through popular images of NGOs working with the poor, disenfranchised and needy especially in the light of the high profile of the aid industry (de Waal 1997: 82). Such sentiments also express an increasingly common realisation that the most important resource which NGOs can use to tackle issues of development are the initiatives, ideas and solutions proffered by people themselves. It is these that have the potential to inform relevant and applicable solutions.

As an anthropologist working in a post conflict area in east Uganda, I have been privy to the ability of people to respond to turbulent events in active and indigenously relevant ways. I conducted fieldwork in the Teso region of Uganda, which has been marred by political conflict for a period of twelve years between 1979 and 1991. Initially this consisted of armed cattle raiding against the people of Teso by their neighbours the Karamojong people. As a result of this raiding huge numbers of cattle, long the source of wealth and productivity in Teso, were lost. In 1986, however, the people of Teso went into insurgency against the then new government in Uganda, the government of the National Resistance Movement under the presidency of Youveri Museveni. An anti government military rebellion was organised. The ensuing fighting was violent and devastating. In 1989, as a move to end the insurgency, Museveni ordered the forced removal of the rural population in Teso into settlement camps. Conditions in the camps led Amnesty International to accuse the NRM government of serious human rights abuses in the Teso area (Amnesty International 1992).

By 1991 the insurgency had dwindled to a close and people were free to return home. The impact of the conflict on the area had been resounding. Infrastructure had been destroyed, agriculture had collapsed and people who left the camps and went home faced conditions of extreme impoverishment. Nevertheless there has been in the years since 1992 a noticeable improvement in Teso. In fieldwork between 1996 and 1998 I was witness to the active coping strategies and initiatives for recovery and reconstruction put into place at a grass roots level. With conditions of peace, people in Teso have been able to pick up the pieces and put their lives together. The place of 'community-based action' as a concept in NGO policy is advocacy of moves to tap into and promote such resilience. The tool of Participatory Rural Appraisal (PRA) fieldwork has opened a practical space in which NGOs can acknowledge the opinions and initiatives of those peoples with whom they work and combine these opinions into the implementation of projects. Implementation itself takes place in two major ways; NGOs can either link with existing Community-based Organisations (CBOs) or they can create new community-based initiatives (Fowler 1997: 94).

LINKING WITH EXISTING COMMUNITY-BASED ORGANISATIONS

When NGOs seek to link with existing CBOs or Grass Roots Organisations (GROs) the sense of 'community' with whom they wish to work is of a unified group of people who already have an initiative, an expression of social capital that can be promoted and managed for development. There is ample witness to the fact that people faced with difficult and oppressive conditions may mobilise themselves into self-help organisations. Lind (1997) has described the communal kitchens set up by women in Lima, Peru in the 1990s.

The introduction of structural adjustment in Peru combined with a period of civil war brought ever-spiralling costs of living and deepening rates of poverty. Rural-urban migration continued apace. In response, women in Lima, activated a wide net work of communal kitchens. As Lind describes it: Every morning, some 40,000 low-income women belonging to the Federacion de Comedores Populares Autogestionarios (FCPA, or Federation of Self-Managed Popular Kitchens) gather at 2,000 sites throughout Lima's poor neighbourhoods, pooling their human and material resources to feed their families, some 200,000 persons.

Twenty to 30 female friends, relatives, church mates and neighbours participate in each comedor. Women are joined by shared concerns and are welcomed in theory regardless of political positions or religious affiliation. The women rotate in positions of leadership and all take turns collecting dues, buying foodstuffs, and preparing the meals, usually in one of the members' kitchens. (1997: 1209) Women in Lima responded and confronted the difficult conditions in which they bring up their families through community-based organisation.

Likewise, other groups of women in South America have mobilised in response to escalating urban violence. For example the Maes de Acari organisation from the Acari slum area of Rio de Janeiro is a group of women dedicated to highlighting and resisting the political violence employed by the government. It was formed by a group of five mothers whose children were abducted and 'disappeared' in 1990. The group continued with active campaigns and has been a major force for solidarity amongst the Acari community (Lind 1997: 1212).

Community-based organisations proliferate in situations of poverty and entrenched inequality. They are also formed in response to crisis events and circumstances. Following severe drought in Senegal in 1984 the village of Zom mobilised as a community to regenerate the local agriculture. Villagers added new topsoil to the land and planted rice communally (Fischer 1994: 131). In Uganda there has often been collective reaction by communities to the devastation of the Aids pandemic. Many villages now have community burial associations who organise the food, water collection, cooking and financial outlay for the ever-increasing number of burials that families have to fund.

CBOs are formed as coping strategies and voices for change that are put forward by people themselves. They are organisations that represent the activity and ability of people to respond at a grass roots level even when disenfranchised and marginalised from formal structures of power. CBOs have many strengths. They are organisations formed from within a community to address the locally perceived needs of that community. They address those needs indigenously defined by the community in sustainable, locally relevant and participatory ways.

The effectiveness of CBOs can be wide ranging beyond the primary goals. Different CBO groups often network between themselves, forging social and economic exchanges that further strengthen the organisations and the members within them. For example in Togo the 'Association of Village Enterprises' co-ordinates various CBO groups and insists on the redistribution of surplus resources amongst the network (Fischer 1994: 132).

In Uganda members of a burial association may, after collectively discussing and taking part in each other's problems, embark on a collective business enterprise, pooling financial resources. In line with the strategic shift that has seen NGOs advocating policies to support and encourage community-based development action, many NGOs now seek to link with and support pre-existing CBOs. The links made between NGOs and CBOs offer many advantages in development work. CBOs can give NGOs a partner organisation that is internal to a community; a partner that is established and relevant, already sustained, already trusted and familiar and already legitimate (Fowler 1997: 94).

When NGOs link with CBOs their partnership is one through which NGOs can access a communities needs, effective action and leadership in apposite ways. In turn CBOs can gain wider funding and recognition through their link with NGOs. However, there are three areas in which links formed between NGOs and CBOs require cautionary attention. First the weaknesses of CBOs as actors in development need to be understood. Lind (1997: 1215) argues that, much as the communal kitchens in Lima have addressed the material needs and straits of the women and their families, they can also be seen as having institutionalised the women in their poverty. Members of groups such as the FCPA now live in a state of permanent dependence on the kitchens. In this way the CBO preserves the status quo.

There still remains a gap between the kitchens as a community response to economic circumstances and state level policy which causes the broader economic structures which underpin conditions in the slum areas. The mechanisms by which communitybased action could inform large-scale development effected on a national and international level are still weak.

CBOs are not an automatic route to empowerment for their members. Often they are a response to events and situations rather than addressing the underlying causes. In linking with CBOs, NGOs need to be aware that these are partners who might be engaged in actions based more on principles of welfare and delivery rather than principles of effecting lasting change.

Second there should be attention paid to the question of whether CBOs represent the interests of all the members of a community. Often CBOs are initiated and coordinated by members of an elite, by members of a certain sector of the population and are not socially all encompassing. They may exclude the involvement and opinions of other social groups in the community. Thus the ideas put forward for development through a CBO may be contested, considered invalid or not even recognised by other people in the same community. For example in 1996 a conference was held in the Teso region of Uganda to bring together NGOs and local CBOs in order to discuss initiatives that might be put in place for facilitating reconstruction in the post conflict environment.

A number of CBOs, dominated by educated men, argued their opinion that the best ways NGOs could facilitate reconstruction in Teso was through the funding of cattle restocking programs. A counter argument was put forward by a local women-run CBO to the effect that cattle restocking would only bring environmental degradation to Teso and that the money would be better spent in rebuilding schools for children. CBOs do not necessarily speak for the community. They are formed as groups that may encode social hierarchies, divisions and differences of opinion within a population of people. This has implications for NGOs who link with CBOs. Whilst such a link often serves to strengthen a grass roots based initiative for development, it may also weight one such initiative or idea over another, a weighting that is potentially divisive and contentious to the population involved.

Third, there are complex management issues involved in making links between NGOs and CBOs. Though the link might be termed a 'partnership' CBOs may often lose their autonomy through a link with an NGO and be subject to different standards of practice, accountability and leadership. As a stronger partner an NGO is likely to impose, however unintended, new standards of management. For example in Teso, following the conflict, a group of former rebel soldiers mobilised themselves into an organisation from which to initiate development projects. For three years they existed as an autonomous group who pooled resources of land and oxen and invested in agricultural enterprises.

The members of the group gained enough money from such projects to support themselves and their families and to establish the organisation on a permanent setting with a rented base. They also employed many hundreds of people from local villages on the agricultural projects. After three years the group wrote a project and funding proposal to a large international NGO based in England.

The NGO accepted and sent representative to visit the CBO in order to cement a more lasting partnership that would extend beyond the funding of a single project. This particular CBO gained many advantages from such a link; gaining larger amounts of capital which they could invest in the projects as well as advice from agricultural experts. However they had also to make many changes in their styles of management. As an autonomous organisation they had employed a fluid style of accountability. Each of the members knew at any one time where more or less all the state of the current financial assets. If one of the members faced a personal or familial crisis and the other members agreed, the resources could be diverted to address it, for example providing expenses at a funeral or to repay a debt. In links with the international NGO such a system was changed into one of written accounts and banking. The leadership of the CBO was ultimately accountable to the NGO for its financial management, no longer to its members.

When NGOs forge links with CBOs they have the potential to reach deep into a community, to address relevant and locally defined needs, in locally appropriate ways with local personnel. These relationships also have, however, the potential to change the balance of influence within a community and for the CBO involved. It can only be beneficial to clarify rather than obscure the power balances that stem from NGO relationships with CBOs. Such a clarification entails a recognition that in linking with CBOs, NGOs may find that it is not a community with whom they work but a group of people with defined set of interests and not so much a community 'partner' but a base within the grassroots locality. Once the actual power dynamics of a particular NGOCBO relationship are known strategies can be put in place for realistic, rather than idealistic management.

CREATING COMMUNITY-BASED ORGANISATIONS

In many situations people at a local level faced with difficult and overwhelming situations do not necessarily form CBOs, even though they may respond to their circumstances with active resilience and coping strategies. In such situations, where there is an absence of potential CBO partners, NGOs have the alternative of a second route for community-based action; they can precipitate the creation of community-based organisations which harnesses the resilience and potential of community inspired action.

Such work has important strengths. It introduces an organisation that is specifically geared towards social change and social needs. In the UK, since the 1960s, community-based work by charities and voluntary organisations has proliferated in response to government policy. Such work has sort to and has succeeded in empowering people in various ways; through the mobilisation of community identity and esteem, through political education, through opening channels by which the poor and marginalised can relate to the state (Taylor 1995: 109). Community-based organisations that are created specifically for development purposes have the advantage of being potentially democratic and unifying agents for change (Fowler 1997: 94). Within such locally based development work the idea that NGOs use of a 'community' is of an ideal unit from which to promote and to manage grass roots, participatory development. Creating community-based organisations and mobilising communitybased action is seen as a way of working with and augmenting local, small scale, social units in relevant ways.

However, it has been increasingly recognised that, in practice, community-based action is often extremely difficult to achieve. The implementation, realisation and management of development which has the concept 'community' at its heart has proved problematic for many NGOs. For example, in the Teso region of Uganda an English based NGO sought to introduce community-based projects for the reconstruction of relations between Karamojong and Iteso peoples after the years of conflict between the two sides. The idea was to set up new communities in previously unoccupied land, communities that consisted of both Karamojong and Iteso peoples who would work together on development projects such as the rehabilitation of roads and bore holes. Four communities were founded with volunteers from each of the two sides, each base had an expatriate member of staff and basic transport provision. In many ways the idea was a success. It saw development work located in remote, up country areas. Many other NGOs concentrated their efforts in Teso near to the town that offered good transport and living facilities for expatriate workers. The communities have also proved to be a source of economic regeneration for other villages in their vicinity, providing access to resources and skilled personnel. However, deep and bitter division still remains between the Karamojong and Iteso inhabitants. One of the bases was forced to close after an armed, violent conflict between members of the community, each side accusing the other of trying to gain stronger political influence in the community. The expatriate worker was rapidly evacuated.

A major problem for the management of community-based action is that the idea of 'community' as advocated in NGO policy is often a simple and romantic notion which is difficult to find, work with and translate into practice. As Guijt and Shah (1998: 7) have noted: the use of 'community' as the unit of analysis for much work that passes as participatory is problematic...it evokes images of meeting people's real need and widespread participation at the grass roots level, thus creating a normative sense of 'a good thing'....inequalities, social hierarchies and discrimination are often over looked and enthusiasm generated for the co-operative and harmonious ideal promised by the imagery of 'community'.

Among NGOs the concept of 'community-based action' is often used to imply an automatic and uncontested translation into development that works at the grass roots level. The concept of 'community' is used to imply the social unit through which NGOs can best engage with the needs of their beneficiaries. Such usage ignores the actual complexity and reality of social relations between people in the same locality, a complexity that might have direct bearing on the success of the development envisioned. The concept of 'community' used in much of NGO development discourse is weak in five major areas. First, it leaves no room for acknowledging the social dynamics between people who live in the same locality. Communities are infused with systems of power, hierarchy, authority and value, which define the lives of their members. These structures can mitigate against a joint and communal undertaking. For example between the Karamojong and Iteso members of the new NGO facilitated villages, there existed strong political and ideological differences as well as a history of hostility. This ensured that it was not possible to create automatically a harmonious community, despite people coming to live together in the same locality.

The social relations between members of the same locality can be overtly hostile and involve conflict. In the Teso region of Uganda, people have returned to their home villages after the years of displacement into camps. There they often find themselves living back next to neighbours or even relations who had inflicted violence upon them during the very personal and local violence of the recent past. Such histories, though not overtly mentioned, are remembered and mitigate against collective reconstruction and development projects. Families tend to work separately to improve their own homes rather than join in communal initiatives. Even in populations with less fraught social relations many NGOs find that when they seek to work in a community they will be drawn to one segment of the population; in rural Uganda those who work most readily with NGOs tend to be the educated, English speaking minority. Others in the population often feel disenfranchised from systems of authority and influence. In addition the usage of 'community' as an ideal concept ignores the fact that there is change over time within the group in question. Anthropologists have long been criticised for taking the communities of people with whom they work as a synchronic, bounded and functioning entities. The shift now is to undertake research that accommodates the historical and changing nature and values within a community of people especially in response to broader contextual events.

It is these dynamics which affect the possibility oi managing community-based development. Payne (1998) has discussed the work of OXFAM in the Ikafe refugee settlement of north Uganda. Sudanese refugees in north Uganda had been encouraged to move to Ikafe out of the transit refugee camps. In Ikafe OXFAM aimed to implement a vision of: a self-reliant population, co-existing with local people in small and well-spaced communities: a refugee population who might eventually live independently of any external assistance. (Payne, 1998: vii)

It was hoped that such a vision would work as an alternative strategy to principles of relief that usually characterises work with refugees. In Ikafe OXFAM aimed to strengthen fragmented communities from the grass roots up, promoting participation, capacity building and thus sustainable development. In the event, however, such aims proved almost impossibly difficult to implement. Whilst in the initial year, 1995, OXFAM made advances in encouraging self sustaining settlement, subsequently the Ikafe population was subject to armed attacks from both Sudanese and Ugandan armed groups. Many of the population fled from the settlement and became subject to the vicissitudes of the political conflict engulfing them. In this context few community-based initiatives could be successful and OXFAM returned to emergency programming. By the end of 1996 most of the OXFAM staff had been evacuated from the area and the population of Ikafe were once again living in transit refugee camps with OXFAM staff acting as service providers for their short term needs. By 1997 the Ikafe settlement was formally closed by UNHCR and the Ugandan government, the majority of the former population had returned to Sudan under duress.

The social relations between those who live in the same locality are complex and contingent. Development projects that are predicated upon a concept of community conceived without recognition of such dynamics might find that the social reality on the ground renders such projects unfeasible. Second, the concept of community as used in NGO policy is weakened by the assumption that community inspired action will be beneficial to all. Allen's (1998) work in Uganda provides a strong counter to such idealisation of community initiatives. Allen conducted ethnographic fieldwork amongst the Madi of northern Uganda. There people were re-settling after years of displacement, again in the context of political conflict in the Uganda/Sudan border area.

Allen suggests that after years of traumatic upheaval Madi people sought communal therapeutic mechanism through witch hunts. In these young women were targeted, killed and tortured in brutal and fatal ways. Allen suggests that such victims were positioned as scape goats for the tensions inherent in the community. Likewise Heald (1998: 9) has suggested that witch hunts amongst the Gisu of west Uganda in the 1960s functioned in terms of the moral self definition of communities at a time when the concept of community was becoming important as a unit of local political organisation. Once again those suspected of being witches were tortured and killed as community leaders sought to eliminate the perceived immoral influences from their society.

What is clear from such examples is that community initiatives work through deeply held systems of belief and perception; they are not ideologically neutral. Though many indigenous community initiatives will not be so fraught as these examples, all will be informed by their social and cultural context. These influence the action undertaken so that all participants are unlikely to be equal partners, and some may be actively discriminated against. Whilst NGO policy advocates 'turning to communities themselves' in the quest for people centered development there needs to be care not to posit indigenous community action with an automatic moral credibility. A naiveté in the dynamics of community life ignores the 'darker side of traditional communities' (Guijt and Shah 1998: 8) and may lead to the institutionalisation of oppression.

Third the use by NGOs of 'community' as an ideal location for development ignores the fact that people themselves might not see the community as very important. Robertson (1967) conducted research in central Uganda in a locality where many families were migrants to the area. There he found that the most important and valued social bonds in the area were not those of 'community' but those of family relationship and of patronage; richer families hired labourers to work for them and this proved an important source of income. Similarly Werbner (1991) has documented the strong ideological associations of 'home' and 'family' above and beyond that of 'community' amongst the Bango people of Botswana.

During my own fieldwork in Teso it was noticeable that people placed strategies for the well being and reconstruction of their households over and beyond those for the community. This was apposite in an area where conflict had been interpersonal and bitter, in some cases involving neighbours, even cousins and siblings, on opposing sides. In the post conflict period relations between people in the area were shot through with feuds and division relating to the conflict.

These mitigated against communal undertakings. When NGOs in the area tried to mobilise participatory community organisations for well digging and the construction of schools such tensions often prevailed and undermined community mobilisation.5 In addition the priority given to the 'community' by people in Teso varied at different times of the year. During the wet/planting season people would concentrate upon their household agriculture and spent most of their time with other family members on their homelands. During the dry season people had more time and money to enter communal beer feasts and occasions. NGOs working in the area found it more profitable to instigate community directed projects during the dry season and even then to timetable meetings in the early morning to avoid competition with beer parties (Deutsche Gesellschaft fur Technischr Zusammenarbeit (GTZ): personal communication). The question to be raised here is one of motivation. If people's locus of motivation is one other than that of 'community' this is likely to cross cut with NGO ideals for community-based action.

Fourth, the concept of community as used in much NGO policy seemingly isolates the community from the broader historical, regional and national context in which it is situated. As evident in the example of the Ikafe refugee settlement, it is this context which will determine the possibility of community initiatives. In Teso the bottom line for the ability of NGOs to instigate people centered development was the context of peace. With peace had come the incorporation of the area into the national political structure with its system of local councils. This system allows NGOs direct access to the grass roots locality and unmediated communication with local leaders (Brett 1996: 210). Those community initiatives which were successfully implemented by NGOs in Teso often depended upon this governmental structure. Rather than an isolated entity a 'community' exists in a web of wider relationships; it is these that are often the greatest resource in development processes.

Finally, an unproblematic use of the concept 'community' ignores the difficulty of definition. For what people see as a community is not always the same as a grass roots locality

The 'deaf community' for example is a self-defined group of people aware of a distinct culture and life style. As a community they have a number of initiatives and organisations to advocate deaf awareness and to seek consolidation between members of the community yet the members are widespread in location. In Teso the most convincing sense of Iteso community I was witness to was amongst migrants from Teso living in slums in the capital Kampala. Iteso immigrants tended to live in the same area and to actively meet and discuss ways in which they could support and further the conditions of their homes and families back in Teso. A large informal network bound the participants together, providing assistance in the gaining of employment and in transferring earnings and communication back to Teso.

Whereas in Teso such members would have been divided by loyalties to kin and location, in the capital city they formed a community of interests. Anderson (1991: 15) has suggested that communities are, most often, 'imagined' entities where members are bound in common reference to ideas and identity. Cohen (1985: 12) has likewise argued that 'community' be defined according to its use and role in people's experience, according to what the members have in common with each other and how they symbolically distinguish themselves from others. Both writers suggest that community be understood as a phenomenological concept, which expresses the members' joint interests rather than their geographical location. Such definition has implications for NGO management.

For it stresses that the concept of 'community' prevalent in NGO policy should be checked against the empirical reality on the ground. As Pratt and Loizos (1992: 37) warn that a physical community is not necessarily 'a natural unit of social co-operation', nor does it imply a convergence of interests and point out the dangers of ... assuming that simply living near to each other automatically leads to something called 'community spirit'. Such an assumption may well lead to problems if certain common interests and characteristics are projected on to a community before there is any real evidence that they exist.

On the other hand the strength of feeling that may lie within an 'imagined community' suggests that, once identified, herein lies a source of social capital and common interest that might provide a base for development processes, for community initiatives and organisations.

IMPLICATIONS FOR NGO MANAGEMENT

A discussion of the dynamics and definition of the concept of community is vitally important for NGOs, for it is these dynamics which constitute the actual environment for NGOs who seek a better working relationship with their beneficiaries. Whilst in NGO policy community organisations and community-based action have often been reified as unproblematic working units, ignoring their dynamics in practice will work to the detriment of proposed development projects. Such discussion leads to some practical suggestions for NGO management. An important initial step is for recognition of the possible complexities of communitybased action. There needs to be recognition that communities are not homogeneous nor simple and uncontested entities and that even CBOs are organisations that encode lines of power and representation. When NGOs recognise such complexity they will be better focused on the social reality of their beneficiaries.

There is potential in the recognition of communities as social groups held together by systems of belief and value, systems which constitute indigenous social capital rather than as groups necessarily bound together by their locality. Second there is a place for ethnographic research by NGOs amongst the beneficiaries with whom they work. Such research is a commitment to the 'emic perspective (Fetterman 1993: 2) on social life as lived and understood by people themselves. Such research would enable NGOs to ground their community projects less in rhetoric and more in terms meaningful to their beneficiaries. Whilst such research is necessarily long term, NGOs have the possibility to link with those who have already done such research in the areas where 'community-based action' is to be implemented or to employ local staff, members of the community, to take part in designing the vision and planning of development initiatives.

Finally NGOs, particularly NNGOs, would benefit from flexible management strategies to accommodate the link between their organisation and existing CBOs and new community-based organisations. With recognition that partnership with an NGO has the potential to change systems of management and power amongst beneficiaries' groups, NGOs would benefit from looking at how the standards of management they expect differ and may conflict with those of their beneficiaries, and how the difference in standards and management culture may be negotiated. Fowler (1997) suggests that the move of NGOs to supporting people's organisations and away from service and delivery will increase into the next millennium. With such a shift the prominence given to 'community' based development will surely continue. The examples and discussion of this paper seeks to stress that such prominence must be founded with practical and managerial scrutiny rather than with generalised development discourse. With commitment to the lived realities and dynamics of community NGOs can move towards community relevant as well as communitybased action.

2

Charismatic Leadership and Second-Line Leaders in Development NGOs

Competent leadership has always been considered vital in every organisation and there has been considerable research on mainstream leadership issues in the corporate sector and in politics. But there has been very little research on leadership issues in the emerging sector of development NGOs. The issue of second-line leadership development is an important one not only for the NGOs themselves but also for the aid industry, the poor and vulnerable people for whom they work and for society as a whole.

This paper investigates and analyses the question of NGO leadership in Bangladesh and UK and the problems NGOs encounter in developing second-line leaders.

Through collection and analysis of data from primary and secondary sources, this document endeavours to relate existing 'leadership research' to the case of NGOs; assess the state of second-line leadership development in NGOs; and recommend possible strategies out for the future. The paper concludes that in spite of the exceptional qualities of many NGO leaders, there has been no systematic approach to the development of successful second-line leadership.

INTRODUCTION

Background

In every organisation and shared effort, competent leadership has always been considered vital and there have been research on leaders and leadership from time to time in various sectors. "However, most attention is given to the visible and influential domains of leadership that form and direct society through the - often allied - powers of politics and of wealth creating businesses. The emerging domain of non-profit or civic leaders and leadership remains relatively unexplored and poorly understood" (Fowler, 2000: 1). Again, most of the research in business and politics has been done in the developed countries without giving adequate attention to the social development leaders in the non-governmental sector who do not aspire to political power, but work to improve the lives of the powerless in the society (Fowler, 2000). Unlike government or for-profit sectors, NGOs have the distinctive mission of social change and they focus on people who have not been brought under either the government or private sector programmes. This mission and related characteristics create distinct management challenges for NGOs (Hailey, 1999). Appropriate leadership is crucial to face these challenges. Like other organisations, NGOs go through various stages of growth and change. There has been very little research to analyse the role and characteristics of NGO leaders at different stages of the organisation.

The characteristics and role of 'charismatic' founder leaders in NGOs and the concern of developing second-line leadership have been two crucial issues during the last ten years of my work with NGOs in the development field. Throughout my work in programme and partnership development and management, capacity building, and research and advocacy, NGO leadership in general and developing leadership capacities at different levels of organisations have been important concerns. Doing a dissertation as part of my M.Sc. at the Centre for Civil Society, provided me the opportunity to do the research on the issues. This paper is based on primary data collected from both Southern and Northern NGOs3 and development experts, review of relevant secondary literature, and reflections on my own experiences.

RATIONALE AND FOCUS

In spite of the successes of 'start-up' stage NGO leaders in the growth, diversity and quality of their work, most Bangladashi organisations is yet to develop second-line leadership. There have also been anecdotal references to the 'charismatic leaders' that they try to maintain status quo through not letting others grow as potential future leaders, that they do not have enough confidence in others, and so on. Some people also say that the issue has not been a concern in most of the NGOs since the beginning. As indicated earlier, there is scarcity of research and literature in this field. Exploring the issues related to charismatic leadership and development of secondline leaders in NGOs is the focus of this paper. "Like the religious leaders start their speech with 'as God has said in the holy book', each meeting in [the NGO] starts with 'as [the founder Chief Executive] has said..." - Staff member of a national NGO in Bangladesh4 The work of Hailey and Smillie (2001) on NGO leadership is one of the very first systematic research in this area which is mostly focused on the characteristics of successful NGO leaders in Bangladesh, India and Pakistan. All the organisations covered in the study are big NGOs with complex management structures. The study does not focus on medium sized, local and more membership type NGOs. Some of the practices and anecdotal evidences show that second-line leadership development has been a challenge for most of the development NGOs irrespective of size, focus and origin.

The above quote from an NGO staff indicates how dependent that organisation is on its founder leader. Some other evidence includes: " The founder leaders do most of the representations in external meetings and forum, and also get directly involved in all decision-making and day-to-day management. These indicate the absence of suitable alternative people in these organisations.

- Many founder leaders get scared when something goes wrong in their personal life (e.g. sickness). One such leader was heard to say to a partner Northern NGO saying, "what will happen to my organisation if I die tomorrow?".
- Some NGO staff members are unwilling to express their opinion even on small issues without talking to their leaders. When a donor asked to revise the annual plans and budgets of a local NGO5, the staff members said, "we cannot do it because [the leader] prepared the annual plans and budgets before leaving for the current foreign tour which was several weeks even before the process started".
- There have been a wide range of complaints from outgoing staff of NGOs about their leaders' unwillingness to let potential staff grow for future leadership roles. According to Fowler (2000), the knowledge gap in the study of leaders and leadership in NGOs may have important consequences for thinking, policies and practice in the development field such as
- It may set unwarranted boundaries around the concepts, frameworks and theories applied to understand how societies generate, appreciate and distribute leadership.

- It limits and may distort the picture of leadership that gives rise to the "actual configurations of civic institutions and organisational behaviours to be found across the world". In a politically weak state with less accountability to citizens, such distortions may "give rise to highly questionable policy recommendations, expectations and programmes of external assistance".
- The perspectives from the business sector increasingly become the reference points and ways to analyse, understand and improve the leadership in societies. The third consequence may create a 'monochrome, if not monolithic' view of the business sector dominating the analysis of leadership. Some analysts argue that leaders in the Third Sector have to make more significant contributions to the organisations than those in the corporate sector6. Despite the lack of research on the reasons for the greater impact of the leaders in voluntary organisations, "the nature and quality of voluntary sector leadership is considered more likely to determine achievement than in other organisations" (Fowler, 2000: 5). Developing second-line leaders (preferably from within the organisation) is a crucial issue in NGO management, but many experts observe that it is not happening in most cases. While developing second-line leaders is important for all organisationsl, it seems even more important for NGOs because:
- NGOs are value driven organisations and there is need to maintain an optimum level of continuity of their vision, mission and values. This can be done effectively through developing professionals from within the organisation to take future leadership role.

- NGOs are known as training grounds for social entrepreneurs with the potential to spread their values in the wider society. This can be done more effectively through creating leadership capacities within the organisation.
- Creation of capable second-line leaders will enable the founder leaders to get involved in more policy advocacy and long-term strategic work.
- The aid agencies have attached high priority to 'capacity building' in the developing countries - both in public and voluntary sectors. Leadership development is a key concern to investigate the capacity limitations in the voluntary sector in the South (IFCB, 1998).

There has been plenty of work on leadership in the business sector and in politics, but hardly any in relation to NGOs. This paper seeks to contribute to filling this knowledge gap, and indicates issues for further research. The paper focuses on development NGOs working in the South, and in particular, Southern NGOs (SNGOs). The reasons for the particular focus on SNGOs are: a) they are more dependent on external resources and vulnerable to the environments which are mostly inhospitable for their work making their "leadership more tricky and, potentially, at personal risk" (Fowler, 2000: 3); b) in a number of countries in the South, many of the founder NGO leaders are now approaching retirement making the development of second-line leaders and succession very critical issues; and c) my own experience of the leadership challenges through my work with local, national and international NGOs in the South.

The purpose of the paper is to investigate and analyse the question of NGO leadership and some of the problems encountered by NGOs in developing secondline leaders.

With this end in view, there are the following specific objectives:

- Relate the existing 'leadership research' to the specific case of NGOs;
- Make an assessment of the state-of-the-art of second-line leadership development in selected NGOs;
- Analyse the factors for being able/unable to develop second-line leadership; and
- Suggest possible ways out for the future and indicate issues for further research.

There are three key queries in the paper: what happened, why and how, and what is the future. In line with this framework, the following specific issues have been addressed:

- The main contemporary theoretical foundations for leadership, and how leadership theories apply to different contexts and sizes of NGOs;
- The main traits of the successful NGO leaders in the South and in the North;
- What happened among NGOs in developing second-line leaders, why and how; and
- Possible ways out towards developing capable second-line leadership and issues for further research.

Some issues and open-ended questions were used to prompt the discussion during the primary data collection.

Methodology

Selection of NGOs: Due to limitation of time and other resources, the SNGOs were selected from Bangladesh and the northern NGOs from among those with headquarters in the UK. The following three categories of NGOs were selected from Bangladesh:

- One NGO with a 'charismatic' male founder leader that is known to have developed second-line leaders.

Bangladesh Rural Advancement Committee (BRAC), which implements integrated programmes in more than half of Bangladesh, was selected for this category.

- One with a 'charismatic' founder leader that is yet to develop second-line leaders. Nari Maitree - working in Dhaka (the capital city) and a few other districts - was selected. It was founded in the 1980s and has been headed by a woman leader. It implements integrated development programme with the major focus on women and adolescents. It has a multi-donor funding base and it has been showing steep growth curve over the last half a decade. One NGO with a more 'membership-type' structure working as a full-fledged NGO since early 1990s (started as a local youth club in the mid 1980s). Young Power in Social Action (YPSA) in Chittagong was selected for this category. It has a relatively young team and works on selected themes e.g. disability, micro-credit, etc.

Leadership, Charisma and NGOs - an Overview

This part reviews the mainstream leadership literature mostly from business and politics. Although neither business nor politics provide an adequate grounding for suitable analysis and interpretation of NGO leadership, this perspective can help expand the boundaries of existing theories and the practices to which they give rise (Fowler, 2000).

This part also compares the studies of leadership from political, economic and civic standpoints, and continues to identify the knowledge gap in the non-profit10 or third sector research on leadership in general and NGO leadership in particular.

Leadership: Definitions and Concepts

Machiavelli (1468-1527) is one of the earliest theorists of leadership who described certain effective techniques for manipulation and remaining in power (including deceit, bribery and murder) that gave him a bad reputation in the later centuries. However, he wrote in the context of Italy of his time, and what he described can now been seen in terms of 'power distance' (Hofstede, 1980). People have defined leadership in many different ways. Winston Churchill called leadership "the intelligent use of power". John Adair suggested that leadership is about "holding people together as a group while leading them in the right direction". ... John Harvey-Jones suggested that leadership was about "getting extraordinary performance out of ordinary people" (Hailey, 1999: 2). From all these definitions some of the key aspects of leadership can be summarised such as: ability to communicate basic rules that make organisations effective (Grint, 1997a), possessing and applying multiple intelligence (Mant, 1997), facilitating others to act together and to excel (Kouzes and Posner, 1995), ability to create followers (Wheatley, 1994), gathering and intelligently using power (Adair, 1990), setting personal examples (Drucker, 1990), and 'holding' and projecting a vision (Fiedler, 1967).

Two major characteristics of leaders emerge out of these aspects:

- the ability to create self-motivation among others without imposing things on them; and
- the ability to align and unite the behaviour of individuals and groups to a direction required for the success of the organisation.

The first characteristic, linked to personality traits and practices that followers value, has claimed a lot of attention. Some experts tried to find specific 'ingredients' of leadership (e.g. Kouzes and Posner, 1997 as quoted in Fowler, 2000). One may argue that once these ingredients are known, people can be trained and made leaders. On the contrary, other evidences suggest that other elements are required to make a leader such as s/he provides a valued purpose and a direction that people willingly follow - these are more linked to psychological needs of followers and to human relationships. This 'direction-giving' quality creates 'transformational' leadership (Burns, 1978).

Mant (1983, 1997) draws on Gardner's (1993) notion of multiple intelligence and argues it is one way to frame all the above aspects of leadership. Gardner talks about seven types of intelligence such as linguistic, logical, spatial, musical, bodily, interpersonal and intra-personal.

Putting further emphasis on the inter- and intra-personal aspects, Goleman (1996) talks about emotional intelligence and asserts that the conventional perspective on intelligence as logical capacity (e.g. IQ) is too narrow; rather knowing oneself and relating to others is crucial for leadership. Mant expands further on this and argues that 'broad-band' intelligence including personal insight in relating to oneself as well as others and a practical understanding of the world is crucial for leadership.

All these characteristics along with "undamaged psychological make up, generate trust and 'followership' around shared, valued goals and ideals". It is important to point out that "broad-band intelligence allied to psychological damage can also produce effective leaders, but with malign agendas that also create significant followership" such as Hitler (Fowler, 2000: 8). Inspirational guidance and value-based goal setting are particularly important for NGO leaders who are dedicated to social change because followership in NGOs does not come as a result of economic incentives and market rewards but as a result of "less tangible foundation of cultural, socio-political values, norms and associated aspirations" (Fowler, 2000: 8).

Leadership Studies

The United States saw a current of growth in leadership theories during the last several decades. Some of the best known were put forth by the late Douglas McGregor (Theory X versus Theory Y, cf. McGregor, 1960), Rensis Likert (System 4 management, 1967), and Robert R. Blake with Jane S. Mouton (the managerial grid, 1978). What these theories have in common is that they all advocate participation in the leader's decisions by his/her subordinates; however, the initiative toward participation is supposed to be taken by the leader (Hofstede, 1980, in ed. Pugh, 1997: 240).

Bryman defines leadership "in the context of a process of social influence whereby a leader steers members of a group towards a goal" (1992: 2). He also examines the main trends and approaches to the study of leadership.

The large body of literature on the mainstream leadership contains the analysis of different dynamics and dimensions of leadership. To some theorists, leadership is dependent on the environment and circumstances suggesting that leadership behaviour is influenced by external and organisational culture, tradition, and social and political elements (Hofstede, 1991).

Much of the literature on leadership suggests that the successful leaders are highly pragmatic, flexible and capable of adapting various leadership styles depending on the needs of situation (Vroom and Yetton, 1973). As presented in the above table, many leadership theorists also focused on the innate leadership traits and skills of leaders in an effort to establish the personal and psychological qualities of leaders in order to distinguish them from non-leaders and followers

(Lynch, 1993). The recent management literature emphasises the role of leaders as the heart of learning process. According to these theorists, leaders should be seen as designers, stewards, and teachers in a learning organisation (Senge, 1990 and Fowler, 1997).

Recently, there have been debates over the usefulness of maintaining a division between the views of leadership as a set of natural qualities or it can be nurtured. Because, while there may be inherited and innate qualities such as 'broad-based' intelligence and intellectual capacity, there are other factors for developing leadership qualities such as experience and learning from one's own life, formal education, etc. Thus, much of leadership qualities are "learnable, but a strong intrinsic potential is a definite asset" (Fowler, 2000: 10). As Peter Senge puts it: "The ability of people to be natural leaders is, as near as I can tell, is the by-product of a lifetime of effort - effort to develop conceptual and communication skills, to reflect on personal values and to align personal behaviour with values, to learn how to listen and to appreciate others and others' ideas. In the absence of such effort, personal charisma is style without substance." (Senge, 1990: 359)

LEADERSHIP STUDIES IN BUSINESS, POLITICS AND THE THIRD SECTOR: A COMPARISON

The principal goal of the leadership research in business is to find and develop people who can improve competitiveness and generate economic value. While the key objective in such research is to find out why and how those people who are preeminent stand out in the creation of 'economic capital' and financial wealth, the efforts aim at prescribing models, methods and guidelines for potential leaders (Fowler, 2000). With such utilitarian purpose and the implicit intention to view leadership and management very close to each other, leadership research in this sector tries to expose and teach how leadership can ensure business profit. While linking leadership with the economic performance, such research also looks at certain human elements and processes such as a leader's psychological characteristics, life shaping experiences, relationships, personal behaviour, etc. However, all these are geared towards the financial profit generation goal of business. An indicator of the dominance of the research and theories from this sector on leadership is the number of books coming to the market with own styles and approaches every year (Grint, 1997a).

The study of leadership in politics tries to investigate and explain an individual's success in terms of his/her "socio-economic origins, psychological characteristics, life-shaping experiences, significant relationships, personal behaviour and political ideology and agenda" (Fowler, 2000: 4). It seeks to analyse how these elements contribute to political leadership in certain contexts of time and place, and this is done in many cases from the perspective of a historian or a biographer. Political leadership may emerge from reactions against certain oppressions, and/or social and labour movements.

The biographies of M.K. Gandhi and Nelson Mandela (Sampson, 1999) are two examples. These studies seldom lead to "prescription in terms of dedicated programmes of individual formation and political advancement or selection" and, in this sense, "political leaders 'arise to the moment', they are seldom formally trained for such roles" (Fowler, 2000: 4). There has been little research and knowledge on the third sector leadership or civic leadership. One indicator of this is the very few journals dedicated to the non-profit leadership and management. Biographies of civic leaders are difficult to find despite their "more substantial contribution to the society than commonly assumed" (Fowler, 2000). Their contributions have been significant in employment creation, contribution to gross domestic product and in size in comparison with industry groups (Salamon and Anheier,1998).

The importance of NGO leadership is increasingly being recognised. Some recent initiatives include:

- The Aga Khan Foundation funded study on the growth of NGOs in South Asia looking specifically at leadership (Hailey, 1999).
- A Ford Foundation funded programme in the Philippines to develop a new generation of NGO leaders (CODE-NGO, 1998).
- The recent research initiated by Alan Fowler on what makes NGO leaders effective, when and how transitions take place, and who the successor generations are and how they are formed (Fowler, 2000).

Nevertheless, these initiatives are few, compared to the vast area of the NGOs and the rich experience of the leaders in this sector all over the world. Leaders and leadership in NGOs remain "an Achilles' heel of capacity building initiatives, be it for social development or political-civic ends" (Fowler, 2000: 6). Simultaneously, it is also clear that there has hardly been any organised initiative so far to investigate the issue of developing second-line leaders in NGOs.

Charismatic Leadership

Max Weber's view of leadership was based on his analysis of political authority and the means by which it exercises legitimate domination. He identified three types of legitimate domination with charismatic domination considered the most powerful social force. Specifically, "charisma is ... the quality which identifies a particular person as a leader in the eyes of those around him" (Mommsen, 1974: 78). Such a leader is able to rally himself a retinue of devoted followers who "... accept his leadership because they believe in his personal qualifications as a leader per se, whatever his particular goals may be" (Mommsen, 1974: 78). For Weber, a major function of such a leader is to ensure that an anonymous bureaucracy does not dominate society, and that the political remains dominant over the bureaucratic (Beetham, 1974: 217).

A charismatic leader can gain the trust of a following. He brings "... the masses behind him by means of the machine" and the members of the constituency are "for him merely political spoilsmen enrolled in his following" (Weber, 1947: 107). With mass confidence, he has the independence and freedom to pursue his own convictions and introduce new social aims. All genuine leaders were perceived by Weber to have some charisma. This he considered necessary to maintain domination. Using their charismatic powers they could sell their goals and objectives to the people at large. This process transforms the personal emotional relationship between charismatic leaders and the followers into a stable and more routine one, whereby charisma becomes routine (Mommsen, 1974: 86). The qualities of a charismatic leader are "... passion, a sense of responsibility and a sense of proportion" (Weber, 1947: 115). They live and work for a cause in which they believe, are practical and have a down to earth view of how to achieve aims, and a willingness to accept responsibility for a policy and its consequences (Beetham, 1974: 95).

The Leadership vs. Management Debate

One of the conventional ways to differentiate between a 'leader' and a 'manager' is by their primary orientation and tasks (Hudson, 1995: 242). "Commonly, a leader is seen as someone who exercises influence over another in the attainment of organisational goals, whereas managerial functions, for example organising or planning, does not necessarily involve leadership skills" (Hailey, 1999: 3). According to Drucker (1955), leaders "lifted a man's vision to higher sights and performance to higher standards" while managers "confirmed day-to-day practices of the organisation". Expanding on this, Bennis and Nanus (1985) say that leadership is path finding while management path following. Management is concerned with "doing things right, whereas leadership is about doing the right things" (Hailey, 1999). Thus, leaders are concerned with inspiration, purpose, organisational positioning, strategy and the future while the managers are mostly concerned with the 'nuts and bolts' of management to achieve the shared purpose of the organisation. There have been criticisms against this kind of separation between the two and some theorists such as Lessem (in Graham, 1991: xvi) have argued that this approach is divisive; it does not emphasise the need to integrate both. According to Kotter (1990), leadership complements management instead of replacing it. He views leadership as a process that creates positive feelings among staff, inspires them and unlocks their potential.

NGO Leadership

As indicated earlier, "there is limited research into the leadership characteristics and managerial capabilities of key individuals, whether they run an NGO or a rural development programme" (Hailey, 1999: 3). In many cases, NGOs are not considered to be led by a senior team in the organisation rather they are seen to be 'owned' by one single leader. Some theorists tend to see leadership as a quality distributed at different levels of the organisation and, thus, everyone in the organisation has a leadership role to play at a certain level and at a certain period of time. According to Grint (1997b) "leadership is a social or collective phenomenon" (p. 140).

This latter aspect is particularly relevant for NGOs as they need to empower their staff to work with the communities (Fowler, 1997). Thus, the NGO staff at different levels of the organisation need to demonstrate their leadership through facilitation in order to develop leadership among the people they work with who are outside the organisational structure. NGO leadership in practice appears closer to the contingency approach as opposed to the view that there is a best way of leading. According to this approach, leadership 'depends' on the respective context, the past and current status, and future goals of an organisation. One important element of this approach is the influence of 'culture' on leadership. As the research on leadership in business goes, various cultural issues (such as norms, conventions, standards, expectations, etc) have significant bearing on leadership (Hofstede, 1991).

Culture is an important element for NGOs as well and it is made more complex by the typical combination of cultural influences from various sources such as from outside, from within the organisation and from abroad (Fowler, 1997). Many NGOs themselves are often forced for political and other reasons, to focus more on problems of poverty than social justice issues and this set of constraints is further linked to NGOs' dependency on resources and their environments. NGOs' high resource dependency leads to their vulnerability to external control and change (Hudock, 1995). Therefore, to cope with such dependencies, NGO leaders need to have a contingency approach.

The staff members in NGOs have not only to communicate the inspiration of leaders but also to uphold it from their respective levels in the organisation. For instance, to work with the communities, the front-line staff have to "grasp and articulate the image of a changed situation and society to those, the 'client's, who must similarly spire to and eventually embody the change" (Fowler, 2000).

This value-inspired aspect of leadership applies to leaders and all other staff in their respective position and situation. According to Wheatley (1994), the inspirational dimension of leadership has to "act as a force field, binding and directing within and beyond the organisation". Thus, one may not be able to draw the dividing line between leadership and management very sharply in the case of NGOs if these organisations are internally empowering which implies significant delegation of authority (Fowler, 1997). Some mainstream leadership theorists have seen leadership also in the context of an organisation's maturity. Schein (1992) argues that organisations are greatly moulded by the founder leaders at the beginning. While the founder leaders may continue to influence over many years, management and leadership styles vary in line with the maturity of organisations.

While Greiner (1972) is one of the first theorists to talk about different stages of growth experienced by organisations in general, Korten (1990) hypothesised that NGOs evolve through four generational stages such as relief and welfare, community development, sustainable systems development, and people's movements. With an emphasis on the founding stage in shaping the future success, Avina (1993) proposes a four-stage lifecycle of an NGO namely, start-up, expansion, consolidation and closeout. Pointing at the high level of NGOs' dependence on charismatic leadership at the founding stage, Kaplan (1996) works out three phases of NGO growth:

(i) the pioneer phase,

(ii) differentiation phase, and

(iii) integration phase.

At the founding stage, organisational systems, and decision making and relationships are mostly personal and informal.

In a warm atmosphere, leadership is held in respect and the staff members are content to follow. Over time, as organisations grow and the staff become more experienced and specialised, needs for structures and procedures gradually become prominent. In many cases, staff in an NGO may no longer be happy just to follow the leader at this stage, commonly leading to a "crisis of confidence in the founder leadership" (Hailey, 1999).

NGO LEADERSHIP - FINDINGS FROM PRIMARY SOURCES

This part presents the findings of the study mainly from primary sources making necessary linkages with relevant findings from the secondary sources. The findings have been organised around nine interrelated issues.

Growth, Achievement and Challenges of NGO Leaders

All the interviewed NGO leaders came to set up for their organisations following the realisation of urgent development needs among the communities. These include the need for long-term development work following the 1971 War of Independence in Bangladesh; demand from the urban poor for specific services on health, education and income generation; and realisation from cultural activities focused on social problems..

Some leaders, also driven by ideas about personal liberation and creativity, saw NGOs as vehicles to develop the individual's potential and ideas. Some - particularly in NNGOs - tried to see the national country staff taking the leading role and responsibilities to develop more ownership at local level. To them this has also been a symbol of expression of personal potential of national staff. Most of the leaders grew, as they worked, mostly through a combination of trial and learning, and formal training mostly on management related issues. Some of the challenges that they faced include leading and managing the evolution of their organisations which were small at the beginning; determining the focus at different stages and difference of opinion within the organisation; pressure from the local power structure and political parties; and the initial suspicion of the communities such as a perceived religious agenda of NGOs. For NNGO leaders, dealing with multicultural teams, and differences and diversities were two main challenges. Their efforts to develop more national leaders were severely criticised because 'liberating one may threaten others'. Some of the challenges and frustrations they faced in developing (national) second-line leaders are:

- opposition from non-national staff due to a sense of personal insecurity.
- willingness to let go and to transfer authority.
- difference of judgements between leaders and others.
- lack of confidence to seize opportunities, take on responsibilities and make some mistakes (and learn from those).

It may be noted that most of the interviewed staff seemed to have informal knowledge of the stories and background of their organisations. Perception about NGO leadership: charisma and other issues Charisma is perceived as a set of focused magnetic qualities that make a leader accepted and followed by the people without questioning. If we look at any of the historical movements, we see someone bringing the ideas and taking them through. Thus it is a set of personal qualities that makes people interested in the ideas about the great possibilities about the future. It is a set of personal characteristics, ideas, magnetism that ensures loyalty from others (e.g. Jawaharlal Nehru in India). Professionalism and charisma are not perceived opposite to each other as "successful charismatic leaders have to continue to change over time in keeping with the needs/

demands of situation and acquire necessary competence". Charismatic leaders are sometimes lonely people; after some time their professionalism (e.g. managerialism, attention to details, etc) may wear out and they may fail to achieve the spread and depth in the organisation, and in turn they may become unfit for the leadership role.

Charismatic leadership is necessary at the beginning of an NGO followed by transformation towards more professionalism. At the beginning of a successful NGO, charisma is higher and professionalism is lower, while at later stages professionalism is higher and charisma is lower. A leader's responsibility is to transform. If s/he tries to maintain charisma forever, leadership capacity is not built in the organisation and the organisation faces difficulty.

As to comparison between NGO leaders and leaders in other sectors, the respondents said that NGO leaders have to be always conscious about responding to social needs. About the environment of NGO leaders the view was: unlike organisations in other sectors, NGOs live in a more protected environment. Both politicians and business leaders are constantly scrutinised, challenged and 'attacked'.

Habitation of NGOs in kinder and less searching environment also limits NGO leaders' growth, competence, and other capabilities. SNGOs and NNGOs have different types of protection. SNGOs work in their own environment and can have a lot of support from own people; many of the founders are considered as 'gurus'. On the other hand NNGOs, in spite of their better funding protection, suffer from lack of immediacy with the environment they work in. While the SNGOs suffer from the weak governance mechanism, NNGOs are under the dual pressure of the impulse from the South and the pressure from the governance (sometimes due to the lack of 'developing' the governance).

In general, the influences on the NGO leaders come from the events and incidents in early life such as the Renaissance, liberation movements (e.g. setting up of BRAC), education, family values and practices, etc. For one of the leaders, apart from the Renaissance and Asian liberation movements, the influencing figures have been Nehru and Gandhi. For him, Nehru provided the ideas of solidarity, citizenship, potential of people in the South (e.g. people in the South can do things themselves), while the ideas of self-respect, non-violent movements for liberation and change, etc came from Gandhi.

THE NGO LEADERS: AS SEEN BY THEMSELVES AND OTHERS

During interviews, the NGO leaders were asked to characterise their own leadership style and the other staff members were also asked to comment on the same of their leaders.

Characteristics of NGO Leaders as Seen by Themselves and Others

Leaders as seen by themselves Leaders as seen by other staff

- Consultative and builders of vision through involving others.
- Effective communicators, and upholders and promoters of the organisation, not of themselves.
- Open minded to change and implementers of change, and committed to quality.
- Democratic and learning oriented.
- Acceptance to others and know how to approach policy level.
- Think and network globally but act locally.

- Motivator, listener and tolerant.
- Receptive to the views from others while do not wait eternally for others if something seems right to do.
- Not only leaders but also professional managers.
- Risk takers, listeners, learners, innovators, patient, flexible and do not dominate.
- Good communicators and diplomats.
- Motivators and guides while friendly, caring and supportive with staff, and have a lot of confidence in them.
- Open minded (and encourages) to criticism and do not dominate.
- Respect and value for others especially for frontline staff and the poor people.
- Strong sense of ownership of the organisation and maintain a good balance between 'hard' and 'soft' style of management.

One of the second-line leaders (who is a potential leader of the NGO in the future) put forward the following characteristics of his own leadership style: participation, listening and observation, going to people once in a while, respecting people, not using abusive language, toughness without being harsh, and belief in human potential. On the contrary, his characteristics as described by other staff are: not an innovator, a good diplomat, good at keeping things in mind and a potential consolidator of the organisation. They also said that he is yet to be tested as a fullfledged leader. None of the staff members had any negative comment about the NGO leaders while they had a number of complains and criticisms about the potential second-liners whom they considered more as managers than as leaders. Each of the founder leaders was found to have gained enormous trust and confidence from others in the NGOs.

Developing the Second-line: What Happened?

To all the respondents, it is essential for NGOs to develop not only second-line but also leadership at different levels for succession. In their view, leadership should multiply leadership. The general view of the majority was that there has not been systematic approach to developing the second-line in most of the NGOs. Specifically about their own organisations, they said that developing the second-line has been an urge since the early days although most of them could not do it due to various constraints. According to the national NGO, it has been essential to meet the future leadership needs of the organisation to uphold and achieve the mission keeping the needs, demands and challenges of time in perspective. The urge for institutional capacity building and achieving donor independence started in that organisation in the early 1970s (i.e. soon after the initiation of its more development oriented work following the 1971 war).

In one of the medium sized NGOs, realisation and urge about developing the second-line came in the mid-1990s realising the fact that there will not be anybody within the organisation to help if the previous problems with other NGOs, government offices or the local power structure repeat. According the NNGO leader, the urge to develop second-line leadership did not come at the beginning in any of the organisations he worked with. But once the issue came to the forefront, it was taken seriously. In one of his previous NNGOs, the current Chief Executive (CEO), the Asia Director, several Country Directors and many key staff were recruited and groomed under his leadership.

The general view is that the picture is mixed. Countries with a large number of NGOs have more options to choose from, leaders may come from within respective NGOs. Countries with a low density of NGOs may not have the potential to have second-line leaders from within. For instance, the Philippines has more discussions about this than Bangladesh. So far, most of the NGOs have taken just an oblique view to succession. It depends on personal initiatives (mostly of the founder leaders), Board (governance) situation e.g. how strongly the founder leaders control the Board, etc. Succession is not an open discussion yet among NGOs and limited investment has been made into developing second-line leadership.

According to Fowler, "it is not uncommon to find an effective NGDO [Non- Governmental Development Organisation14] leader without a strong second cadre or successor generation. There is also the consideration that a leader may not want a too strong, younger second cadre because it poses a threat to their own leadership position. Such insecurity would be a prima facie indicator of insecurity and hence of possible psychological 'damage'. Inevitably, this is an unwelcome precondition when it comes to leadership transition and organisational regeneration." (Fowler, 2000: 11) Some of the general staff were quite critical about what happened. As they said, NGOs have developed working managers not second-line leaders. They continued:

(a) second tier was created, "to maintain power through creating groups of staff around each of them, and divide and rule through using the factions";

(b) mechanisms are not in place to develop 'human care' attitude among the current second-liners; and

(c) one common concern of staff is "what will happen" after the current (founder) leader.

One of the mid-level staff said, "a common joke in the organisation is that on the following day of [the founder leader's] departure we will come to work wearing helmets to protect ourselves from the stones of rival staff groups".

According to Fowler (2000), only "a few NGOs have "well developed schemes to identify and invest in the necessary experiential exposures to their staff: what business would refer to as career planning and development" (p. 10).

Developing the Second-line: Achievements and Constraints

As to achievements, most of what were put forth were general management capacity building initiatives for staff at different levels. There was only one example where the potential future leaders were given necessary exposure and adequate freedom to leadership role, to 'make some mistakes' and learn from those. Some of the common achievements mentioned include:

- Donor funded institutional capacity building projects, exposure visits and training of staff on thematic issues (e.g. gender planning);
- Work division, decentralisation and delegation.
- Creation of readers' circles and other ways of formal and informal sharing and learning.
- Identification of interest and potential among staff, and providing them required input (such as training) and responsibilities to see how they do.
- Promotion of staff from different levels, and gradual growth of staff capacity in the areas of strategic planning and networking.

The NNGO leader, in most cases, created 'space and opportunities' for people instead of guiding them through (by 'holding their hands'). To him, to develop secondline leadership, one has to remove the bureaucratic barriers. On the contrary, bureaucracy can also be a kind of protection for some people as it provides the 'safety net' of rules and regulations. While talking about the challenges and constraints, he said that the efforts to develop more second-line and national leaders were seen by many as tyranny because liberating one may threaten others. While he pointed at the general challenges and frustrations mentioned earlier, some of the specific challenges and constraints he faced in this are the following:

- Promoting someone for leadership may mean 'depriving' someone else. In such cases, one has to apply own personal judgement (a kind of arbitrariness) that may cause discomfort and frustration among some members of staff.
- The issues of fairness and unfairness rise very strongly, and a leader faces the challenge of judging how much 'unfair' s/he can be for the greater 'fairness' for the future.
- According to the national NGO leader(s), one of the main challenges in developing alternative leaders has been the loss of potential leaders as they left to join other development organisations. The positive aspect of this apparent loss of staff is that
- the organisation has been providing trained human resources for the NGO movement in Bangladesh". Right now many NGOs are being led by ex-staff of that NGO. Some other common major constraints mentioned by almost everyone in the SNGOs were:
- Staff are good at implementation but they lack presentation and communication skills, and confidence while they also do not get the scope to share ideas and learning with others. These are mostly due to the pressure of implementation.
- Lack of appropriate training opportunities and resources for competitive remuneration and other staff benefits. These along with lack of personal

commitment by some potential staff result in high turn over.

- Lack of visionary thinking among staff coupled with the inability of some leaders to disseminate their visionary thoughts among the 'followers'.
- Unpredictability of the future in general; while some NGOs made contributions to other organisations to develop second-liners, but did not look at themselves much.
- Psychological blocks around issues such as the Governing Body and, resource dependent.
- Lack of leaders' confidence, professional capacity, exposure to other organisations / sectors, and extreme sense of 'ownership' leads to repulsion of 'new blood' in NGOs which in turn blocks the development of second-line leaders.

In spite of all the challenges and constraints, the unanimous view was that a strong second-line provides ample time to leaders for reflection, policy work and strategic thinking leading towards sustainability of the organisation and its impact.

Developing the Second-line: External Factors

Both presence and lack of donor financial support for developing the second-line topped the list of the SNGO respondents. A few said that there was no pressure from any donor to develop second-line leadership. The NNGO leader: a) received a lot of support from the partner organisations in the South, while faced resistance from the overseas head office and regional offices mainly due to the sense of personal insecurity of the staff there; b) received a lot of encouragement from the CEOs who allowed ample flexibility and 'controlled chaos'; and c) sensed some scepticism from other NNGOs about the appropriateness and success of the approach of national capacity building and national leadership development initiatives.

The Future: Leadership Issues

One set of respondents' views can be summarised as:

(a) NGOs require different styles over time which may not be coming from the same person - 'clones' of today's leaders may not be required in the future;

(b) how far the 'clones' of the current leaders are required is an issue to see over time; and

(c) it is also important to see who defines the situational characteristics of the future leaders. The views of the founder leaders were:

- The future leaders should have appropriate leadership personality to prevent potential factions in the organisation, they should be more consensus-oriented (instead of power), and they should play facilitators' role at different levels of the organisation to uphold and achieve the mission which should remain the same over time.
- The future leaders have to have high acceptance, have to be 'better' than the current leaders and more flexible in dealing with the rapidly changing environment. They also have to be impartial and remain above politics (to manage the potential factions in the organisation).
- There is no major threat in developing the future leaders as all staff members are involved in everything; tensions may arise if 'outsiders' or 'juniors' are brought in to the overall leadership role.
- The next generation will need to deal with the pressure from the environment such as local

leaders and politicians. Development is a political process and NGO leaders have to play important role without getting involved in party politics.

- Future leaders have to have a twofold approach to programmes e.g. basic needs fulfilment, and policy advocacy to ensure rights and entitlements for the poor.
- Today's leaders have to leave a 'virtuous spiral' for the future. Although all the NGO leaders were quite optimistic about the future and had plans for appropriate leadership capacity building along with succession planning, they were also aware of some threats such as:
    * there may be a lack of dynamic leadership;
    * donor reluctance to fund such activities;
    * potential psychological factions among the second-liners and consequently among other staff; and
    * difficulty in dealing with the issue of political identity of NGOs.

THE FUTURE: OTHER ORGANISATIONAL ISSUES

All the founder leaders envisioned their respective NGOs to remain one organisation in the future and keep growing while all the respondents had the common view that a 'clone' of the current organisational set up may not be required. Some of the specific plans for the future include:

(a) reduction of external resource dependency through local resource generation to facilitate development of second-line leaders;

(b) the organisations will continue to grow and innovate while there may be needs to merge some programmes;

(c) the governance structure has to have better mix of disciplines and the members will need to involve and contribute more;

(d) the organisational structure will need to play more facilitating roles; and

(e) more consolidation of programmes may be required along with enhancement of the sense of 'ownership' among staff.

The view of the NNGO leader may summarise a major part of the future organisational issue of NGOs: not a monolithic organisational structure or leadership style - these must be more situational. In the changing environment there will be needs for new organisational arrangements (e.g. merger, acquisition, mutation, etc), new ideas, changes and so on. An NGO has to constantly develop its staff, governance, donors and other constituencies to prepare for the changes over time. One SNGO staff said that if the NGO fails to develop appropriate leadership for the future, the organisation may be taken over by the government.

RECOMMENDATIONS FOR DEVELOPING SECOND-LINE LEADERSHIP

When asked what an NGO should do to develop second-line leadership, the respondents made the following recommendations:

See second-line leadership development as a long-term process so that necessary adjustments and changes can be made in the process e.g. when there are shocks from resource dependency and other factors in the environment.

Discussion, Conclusions and Recommendations

This part presents a discussion on the linkages of the study findings with the existing leadership theories presented in the previous chapters. It also draws some conclusions based on the findings from both primary and secondary sources, and the

- Staff capacity building at different levels leading towards more delegation of authority and responsibility.
- Understanding and analysis of respective national heritage along with a sense of history and change (social, political, etc) - i.e. knowledge of the evolution of own history - along with consciousness about the context and environment.
- Creation of space for second-liners to develop without 'holding their hands' to guide them, rather allowing them to 'make some mistakes' and learn from those).

It ends with a set of recommendations for the development of secondline leaders in NGOs and for further research.

DISCUSSIONS AND CONCLUSIONS

If we compare the findings with the definitions and characteristics of leaders and leadership (discussed in the second part of the paper), each of the NGO leaders are found to possess most of the leadership characteristics to a large extent. They conform to the two major traits of leaders i.e. they are able to: a) create selfmotivation among others around them, and b) align and unite the behaviour of individuals and groups to a direction required for the success of the organisation.

As already indicated above, NGO leaders demonstrate a combination of the various approaches and core themes of leadership over time with a major share of the contingency approach. This is further linked to their ability to ensure survival, growth and diversification of their organisations while constantly responding to the changing needs of the poor and vulnerable.

The founder leaders also demonstrate a strong flair for experiment and learning. Quoting Korten (1990), Lovell (1992) characterises BRAC as a learning organisation and says that its "extraordinary success in rural development has been attributed to this basic feature of its operational mode". They also maintain that: "BRAC 'learns as it goes' through a responsive, inductive process, and that programs grow out of village experience because BRAC is strongly participative" (Lovell, 1992: 4).

Each of the founder leaders was found to have charisma to various degrees, and neither themselves nor other staff members found this as a negative aspect of their leadership. Young (1995) can be referred to in this connection who says, "successful international associations feature a special brand charismatic leadership". Commenting on charisma, he points at "leaders who can inspire, encourage, support and set examples". The NGO leaders in the study have been able to create effective followers who accept their leadership because they believe in their personal qualifications as leaders. In the eyes of the other staff in those NGOs, the leaders also have very good managerial capacities along with strong sense of 'ownership' of the organisations (comparison can be made with Akhter Hameed Khan16 in Khan, 1999). Without directly blaming the founder leaders, everyone talked about the inability of the organisations to develop appropriate leaders for the future. As presented earlier, most of the respondents feel that those NGOs have developed effective second-line managers, not leaders.

Dependency on the founder leaders was clearly visible in every organisation. In one hand this may be due to the long tenure of the founders and not allowing the staff from the second-line to take some major leadership role so that they can equip themselves for future leadership role while the other staff also gain confidence in them. According to Chambers (1997), these leaders can achieve a lot of things through their "guts, vision and commitment" but their power is a disability that hinders organisational effectiveness. He also argues that such leaders are "vulnerable to acquiescence, deference, flattery and placation". As they are "not easily contradicted or corrected", they may get easily tempted "to impose their own agenda, block change and deny the realities and perceptions of others" (Hailey, 1999). On the other hand, the time bound nature of leaders in NNGOs has the potential to limit long-term 'charismatic domination' and push to develop or attract alternative leadership. Although there have been references to the detrimental role of these leaders as 'charismatic autocrats' or the 'guru syndrome', these leaders are the people who - dealing successfully with various political, financial, developmental and managerial challenges - have made their NGOs "exemplars of a new type of organisation that is beginning to change the face of South Asia" (Hailey, 1999). Overall, the job of an NGO leader is complex. According to Fowler (2000: 12), "it involves making correct external and internal value-based 'readings', reaching sound judgements and producing the right decisions" about "specific features of a multi-layered sociopolitical environment", "inspirational civic agenda", and appropriate organisation "to bring about the envisioned change". Emphasising the need for multiple intelligence and qualities such as "constant, conscious practical attention founded on broadbased intelligence, personal insight, interpersonal skill, intuition and agility", he proposes the following definition for NGO leadership:

> *"The art of sound judgement and process of achieving self-willed social change through others within and beyond the organisation".*

According to Hailey (1999: 2), these leaders are able to "balance their values and aspirations, with technical competencies and environmental analysis". Based on his recent research on NGO leadership in Bangladesh, India and Pakistan, Hailey concludes that the leaders of successful NGOs (all of whom have been leading their organisations since the start-up stage):

> *"are pragmatic, rational, and aspirational. ... have aspirations to help the poor, a desire to build sustainable communities, and a set of values that believe strongly in participative, inclusive approaches to development. They recognise the importance of communicating with individuals, motivating teams and building coalitions. They are rational knowledgebased leaders who are willing to take the best from science and education, to apply contemporary skills and competencies, and continue learning and relearning. ... they have also developed an understanding and insight into the environment in which they work. They have the analytical ability to react [to] changing circumstances, to apply appropriate judgement, and respond to the moment" (Hailey, 1999: 10).*

In the words of Uphoff (1998: 50), these leaders are effective because of their "conviction and consistency regarding the potential of the rural people", while Fowler (1997: 75) points at their "adherence to moral principle" and their "enduring, consistent drive, rather than charismatic personality". But, in spite of all their qualities as founder leaders of successful NGOs, those organisations are yet to develop successful and 'tested' second-line leadership. Finally, the existing theories and concepts of leadership are not adequate to address the critical issues of development of societies where NGOs operate. To be complete, current leadership theories need to look at the issues relevant to NGOs from within the sector.

Recommendations

The study makes the following recommendations for developing second-line leadership in NGOs and areas for further research. These are mostly based on the discussions with the respondents, analysis of the secondary information, and my own experience.

- Continuous appropriate capacity building at different levels of NGOs to encourage more delegation of authority and responsibility.
- Understanding and analysis of organisational heritage and context by all staff members and linking these with the causes of poverty and vulnerability.
- Creation of a sense of history and change (social, political, economic, etc) among staff. In other words, developing the knowledge of the evolution of personal and organisation's own histories - along with a consciousness about the context and environment.
- Creation of space for second-liners to develop without 'holding their hands' to guide them, and allowing them the room to 'make some mistakes', get 'tested' and learn from those.
- See second-line leadership development as a long-term process so that necessary changes and adjustments can be made over time particularly when there are shocks from the environment.
- Try out time-bound leadership tenure with strong positive role played by the governance structures.

As to further research, there should be in-depth studies on the aspects related to NGO leadership such as:

(a) capacity building,

(b) sustainability,

(c) gender,

(d) resource dependency,

(e) good governance,

(f) succession,

(g) formation of the leadership and management styles of the leaders (i.e. where they derive their styles from and how),

(h) how NGO leaders extend leadership to the communities,

(i) social innovation and creation of social capital, and

(j) power and control over various processes (e.g. financing, staffing, governance, etc) in NGOs.

3

Combining Service Delivery and Advocacy within Humanitarian Agencies

This paper analyses the strategies of four humanitarian agencies which have been engaged in humanitarian work in Sri Lanka since the start of the war in 1983 and explores the ways in which humanitarian agencies engage with the combatants in a 'complex political emergency'. The paper focuses on the challenges and dilemmas which these agencies have faced in relation to the two sets of combatants: the Sri Lankan government and the Liberation Tigers of Tamil Eelam (LTTE). Focusing the period from 1995 to 1998, the study draws on case data on two Norwegian non-governmental organisations Forut and Redd Barna, and two British NGOs Oxfam and Save the Children Fund (UK).

INTRODUCTION

This paper discusses the strategies which humanitarian agencies adopt when they take up the challenge of advocacy in addition to service delivery. When agencies engage in advocacy the potential for confrontation with the combatants increases. Consequently, access to populations in need may be jeopardised. The paper identifies mechanisms for balancing service delivery with advocacy. I also discuss organisational implications of moving beyond service delivery. The paper is based on extensive interviews with several humanitarian agencies working in the North of Sri Lanka.

Internal Displacement and Response Strategies

Since the war between the Liberation Tigers of Tamil Eelam (LTTE) and the Sri Lankan government started in July 1983, people have sought refuge in safer areas in Sri Lanka, India and the West. In the 1990s the number of displaced people in Sri Lanka fluctuated between roughly 500,000 and 1 million. In addition, an estimated 600,000 Tamils have left for India and the West (Gunaratna 1998: 301). Compared to the 1981 census figures, which put the number of Tamils at a little more than 3 million, these figures mean that half the Tamil population has become either displaced or refugees.

It has been argued that humanitarian aid is in crises and that agencies need to rethink their responses and strategies. One argument maintains that humanitarian aid agencies should 'stick to the knitting', that is remain strictly humanitarian, and the key concern of the agencies should be the needs of the recipients (Halliday 19971, ICRC 1996). This is a view which has been coined 'humanitarian minimalism' (Slim 1997a: 2). According to this view NGOs should develop standards and codes of conduct for their work in conflict situations in order to deal with problems of neutrality and impartiality.

The opposite argument says that humanitarian agencies have to widen their focus in three respects. Firstly, they should link relief and development (IDS Bulletin 1994, UNHCR 1995). Secondly, agencies should work towards integrating relief with human rights and conflict resolution, and make sure that aid does not fuel the conflict dynamic

(Anderson 1995, 1996). Thirdly, their service delivery work should be complemented by lobbying and advocacy work (Clark 1991, Penrose 1994, ICRC 1999). In this paper I discuss the implications for humanitarian agencies of this third proposition.

The Delivery of Humanitarian Assistance in Sri Lanka

The humanitarian agencies in Sri Lanka have been implementing a 'cross line' operation from the mid-1980s. Humanitarian aid has been brought in from government-controlled areas and reloaded at the Forward Defence Line, which demarcates the areas under government control from areas under the control of the LTTE. Once inside LTTE-controlled areas, aid has been distributed jointly between the local administration, foreign humanitarian agencies and local organisations.

The relief operation has over the years been characterised by stability and the large agencies operating in the North have been the same throughout the conflict: Oxfam, Save the Children Fund (SCF), Redd Barna, Forut, Care, Médecins Sans Frontières (MSF), the United Nations High Commissioner for Refugees (UNHCR) and the International Committee of the Red Cross (ICRC).

The LTTE and the government agree on the overall framework for provision of assistance to displaced and economically affected people. Tamils living in LTTE held areas are considered Sri Lankan citizens both by the government and by the LTTE. Both parties agree that it is the responsibility of the Sri Lankan government to provide assistance to them. From the government's point of view, this arrangement secures government links with the population in LTTE-held areas. From LTTE's point of view, government involvement and responsibility ensures that the LTTE does not have to carry the responsibility for providing aid to the displaced population.

Consequently, the Sri Lankan government has played an active role in delivering services during the conflict. It has provided dry rations to war affected people, although the amounts which have been delivered have often fallen short of international standards. When asked, government officials argue that rations are delivered to 'win the hearts and minds' of the Tamil people and to maintain a government presence in the North. On the other hand, the government is concerned that aid may fall into the hands of the LTTE. Supplies are therefore kept at a minimum and agency access is severely restricted.

The administration in the North of Sri Lanka consists of a skeleton government presence and an LTTE 'shadow' administration or departments. This 'dual' administration constitutes a de facto LTTE-administration. The 'shadow' LTTEadministration carries out its own activities and monitors the activities of the government, the foreign humanitarian agencies and the Tamil people. LTTE effectively controls the activities of the government administration through subtle influence, backed by force and brutal assassinations. The government administration has restricted its operations to distribution of relief and the payment of salaries and pensions and an economic embargo has effectively kept economic and developmental activities in the North at a minimum level.

During the early 1990s the LTTE built up its relief arm, the Tamil Rehabilitation Organisation, which was administered under the political wing of the LTTE. The LTTE saw the role of TRO as one of co-ordinating the humanitarian agencies in the Vanni as well as implementing its own relief work. Agency policies with regard to TRO range from rejection of implementation through TRO in principle, to pragmatic implementation through TRO on the grounds that TRO is the most effective implementing agency. In the middle are some agencies which implement through TRO in order to maintain a good working relationship with the LTTE:

In order to maintain the understanding with the LTTE, all the INGOs have chosen to appease the TRO to some extent by letting some projects be implemented by them...If one chooses to implement all projects oneself, the TRO will be dissatisfied and problems may occur with local authorities [LTTE]. If too many projects are implemented by TRO, this will be problematic in relation to the government who regards TRO involvement as having close ties with the LTTE. In other words working in the Vanni involves a difficult balancing act between the two authorities.

The agencies have a multifaceted relationship to the LTTE. On the one hand, they generally have a good working relationship in terms of security arrangements. They are also often able to agree on priorities for the work of the agencies. On the other hand, agencies often experience undue pressure from the LTTE. Firstly, LTTE wants the agencies to bring in as much material resources as possible and to use the resources in areas, and for projects, which the LTTE suggests.

Secondly, LTTE applies pressure on the agencies to persuade them to implement through local organisations. The LTTE exerts this pressure through the NGO consortia and pressure on local agency staff, as well as through meetings between the LTTE leadership and the agencies in the Vanni. Despite this pressure, all the agencies have what they call 'working relationships' with the LTTE which involve different degrees of communication and dialogue with the LTTE.

Some agencies, such as UNHCR, actively seek a dialogue with the LTTE. Other agencies prefer to avoid contact with LTTE as much as possible. Negotiations and compromise Negotiations and compromise is a strategy which agencies employ to manage their day to day relationship with the combatants.

This strategy is based on the existence of an area of common interests between the agencies and the combatants. As pointed out by the head of one of the agencies: I draw this little picture. This is the government's interest. It is big. It is omnipresent, especially in Sri Lanka. An NGOs interest is smaller and parts of it overlap. Where we can work with the government is where we overlap. Where we can go into the uncleared area a force to be reckoned with is the LTTE. Believe it or not, the interests of the government and the LTTE overlap. There is food. There is agriculture. The only place where we can operate in the uncleared areas is where all the three of those intersect...and it always changes. When it is peace that area gets bigger. Agencies respond to pressure from the LTTE by engaging in dialogue or negotiations with the LTTE at different levels, depending on the issue.

Negotiations often take place with the political leadership. The outcome of the negotiations falls into three categories. Firstly, a compromise may be reached between the agencies and the LTTE whereby the agencies, for example, agree to implement certain projects through TRO. Secondly, faced with unacceptable pressure, agencies may decide to withdraw from a local area until the LTTE accepts agency conditions. Thirdly, agencies resist LTTE pressure and the LTTE backs down. Another approach to LTTE pressure is to avoid being pressurised in the first place by designing 'unattractive' projects. This means that the projects do not involve resources which are attractive to the LTTE.

On some occasions the agencies have confronted not only pressure, but incompatible demands from the two parties to the conflict. When hundreds of thousands of people were displaced from the Jaffna peninsula and into the Vanni following the government's offensive against Jaffna town in the fall of 1995, the LTTE pressed for long term agency operations in the Vanni. The government only wanted temporary aid in the Vanni and prioritised rehabilitation in Jaffna. At the time, the agencies chose not to start any long term rehabilitation activities in the Vanni. Neither did they start any large scale operations in Jaffna. An example of how potential reactions from the combatants may stifle agency action and lead to inaction, as predicted by Scott (1995) is given in the quote below:

What we have not been able to do is to study those household coping strategies. We have not known exactly how to do that. The other is...it is very political. All of a sudden you start telling that this has been going down. The LTTE is going to want this to go this way, and the government wants to argue that it is up this way (refers to chart).

As this quote demonstrates, some agencies have been careful in terms of researching and describing the situation knowing that the results will be controversial. As a result, the agencies' work has been based on less accurate information then it would have been, if the agencies had risked going into these controversial issues.

Managing the Relationships: a 'Balancing Act'

All of the agencies claim that they adhere to the principles of impartiality and neutrality in their work. Of these two concepts, the concept of impartiality seems to be the most straightforward to operationalise. Impartiality relates to the relationship between the agencies and their beneficiaries. It means that aid should be provided on the basis of need only, without taking into account any other factors, like race, sex, age, beliefs, etc. Neutrality is important in defining the relationship between the combatants and the agencies, and it is a much more problematic concept to operationalise.

However, a key element is not to take sides in the conflict. In other words, to balance the relationship to the two sides. The way in which the agencies conduct their field operations is one element in the operationalisation of neutrality which I discuss below. All of the agencies agree that an important aspect of maintaining neutrality is to work with both the Sinhalese and the Tamil communities.

So, for example, agencies, such as Oxfam, Forut and UNHCR, which started out by working only in the North have all established programmes in Sinhalese areas as well. Secondly, all the agencies agree that transparency is important in the sense that the government and the LTTE should be kept informed about the activities of the agencies. The emphasis on transparency also prevents misunderstandings between the agencies and the combatants. Thirdly, agencies have different policies in terms of how they implement their projects and programmes. Only two of the agencies working in the North of Sri Lanka are self-implementing: Forut and ICRC. Both of these agencies argue that self-implementation is a necessary requirement for remaining neutral vis à vis the combatants. The other agencies argue that by implementing through local organisations they help build local capacity. They also argue that funds that are channelled through local organisations are closely monitored. UNHCR and Care are the two largest agencies operating in the North and also the two agencies which routinely implement through TRO. Both these organisations argue that they implement through TRO for effectiveness reasons. Oxfam has also implemented through TRO, but only as an exception from the general policy of trying to avoid NGOs which are closely linked to the LTTE.

Fourthly, the agencies have had different policies in terms of how they should work with rehabilitation in areas which have come under government control after having been held by the LTTE. ICRC argues that it would be contrary to the principle of neutrality if the organisation were to start rehabilitation work in areas which had been formerly held by the LTTE, like Jaffna. Oxfam and Redd Barna have had different reasons for not starting work in Jaffna. Oxfam did not feel any need to balance its portfolio by going into more projects in government-held areas. Redd Barna could not accept the conditions laid down by the government which went contrary to Redd Barna policies.

At last, the issue of whether or not the agencies have employed expatriate staff is important. It is assumed by the agencies that expatriates are in a better position to resist pressure from the LTTE. In line with their policies of transferring responsibility to local staff, both Redd Barna and Forut have had a policy of having very limited expatriate staff in their office in Colombo. The other agencies have employed expatriate staff in the field to a much larger degree. UNHCR and the ICRC have adopted different approaches on four out of the five indicators above. Being self-implementing, ICRC does not become involved with the combatants in implementing its relief programme while UNHCR works very closely both with the government and TRO.

UNHCR seems to successfully balance its close relationship to TRO, and frequent meetings with the LTTE, through close collaboration with the government. Both agencies also have a relatively large number of expatriate staff employed in the North and the East. Another factor is that UNHCR and ICRC have by far the largest service delivery programmes in the North and the East of Sri Lanka. Consequently, it is in the government's interest to maintain a good relationship with these two actors. The two Norwegian NGOs differ from the other NGOs on two points: selfimplementation and the use of expatriate staff in the field. Forut, like the ICRC, is the only other organisation that thinks that self-implementation is necessary to remain neutral. During the time when it was doing relief work, Redd Barna was also self-implementing. On the other hand, Care has relied on the opposite strategy which has been to implement through TRO and local NGOs. The government has been concerned about the lack of expatriate staff in the field which was made a requirement for permits to work in Jaffna, after large areas of the peninsula came under government control.

There are also other factors which are relevant to neutrality but which are not a part of the field operations of the agencies. One point which was repeatedly brought up by non-Norwegian NGOs was the 'Norwegian connection'. The Norwegian connection could be defined as the connection which Norwegian NGOs have had to Norwegian aid policy, foreign policy and Norwegian refugee policy. Norwegian foreign policy towards Sri Lanka has emphasised the need for peace and reconciliation. There is also a relatively large Tamil community in Norway. These two factors have been coupled together in the Sri Lankan media to create an image of Norway as a country which would intervene in the peace process on the Tamil side4. Below I want to discuss advocacy as one way in which humanitarian agencies can move beyond service delivery. I have argued above that service-delivery is based on collaboration. Advocacy, on the other hand, increases the risk of confrontation with the combatants.

Advocacy: Risking Confrontation

Conflicts are often characterised by grave human rights violations. According to the former UN High Commissioner for Refugees, Sadako Ogata: Violations of human rights are major - indeed, the major - cause of mass population displacement. This fundamental relationship is not always given adequate recognition... In many ways it would be more accurate to describe refugees as people whose human rights have been seriously violated or threatened (UNHCR 1995:58).

A fundamental change in agency policies took place in the early and mid-1990s. SCF and Redd Barna changed their policies from having relief and development at their core to a focus on children's rights. Oxfam began to put more emphasis on advocacy within the framework of Oxfam's definition of basic rights. These shifts have meant that the agencies have taken up a mandate which would involve some degree of advocacy work as part of a strategy to promote children's rights or the rights of internally displaced people. The shift towards protection and rights based issues have had implications for the role which the agencies play vis à vis the combatants. From concentrating on service delivery, the agencies have had to define an advocacy strategy, both at the local, national, and international level. An advocacy role potentially brings the agencies into conflict with the government and the LTTE as they work to promote the rights of their beneficiaries and other war affected people. Forut has travelled a different path from the other agencies as Forut has always had advocacy for human rights and peace as part of its mandate. From early on in the conflict, Forut played an active role in supporting peace and reconciliation efforts internationally, as well as being active in the European NGO forum.

It is interesting to note that studies among displaced people have shown that they think foreign agencies should play a role in terms of advocacy for peace. Some of the local NGOs also state that they think that the foreign NGOs are in a position to play an advocacy role in relation to the situation for internally displaced people and that they should do so. Among the foreign NGOs there is a tendency to say that the UN is in a better position to play an advocacy role then they are. In other words, the responsibility for advocacy and more confrontational politics is pushed over to other organisations. Within a humanitarian context, Médicins Sans Frontières defines advocacy in the following way:

Being present among the victims and speaking out about their plight in order to improve their basic living conditions and to protect their fundamental human rights (Milliano 1996: 13). As the above quote demonstrates, humanitarian agencies are often present among the victims of violations of humanitarian and human rights law. Consequently, they have access to information about these violations, and the question which the agencies are faced with is: what should they do with this information? What is the case in favour of advocacy?

One of the agencies working in Sri Lanka has argued for advocacy in the following way:

Because if you only pursue one thing the chances are that you end up in really dirty circumstances. That you are only delivering services, but you fail to witness. But if you only witness and not deliver any services, what is your legitimacy in the eyes of the local people who are suffering? UNHCR has developed an overview of human rights and humanitarian law which would be applicable to situations of internal displacements. UNHCR divides human rights into two categories: rights which can be derogated and rights which can not be derogated (UNHCR 1996).

The Sri Lankan government is a signatory to the Geneva Conventions of 1949, in which article three deals with internal armed conflict, but not to the Additional Protocols of 1977 which treat internal armed conflict in more detail. The Government has taken several legal and institutional steps to improve its human rights record. However, following operation Riviresa to capture Jaffna in 1995, extrajudiciary executions, "disappearances", torture and arbitrary arrests continued to take place under the Prevention of Terrorism

Act and Emergency Regulations (Amnesty International 1996). In February 1988, the LTTE declared its commitment to act in accordance with humanitarian law at all times. As for the LTTE's pledge to abide by humanitarian law, Amnesty International have listed a series of areas where the LTTE have acted in breach of international human rights and humanitarian law (Amnesty International 1995: 2). In connection with the visit, in May 1998, of the UN Special Rapporteur on Children, Olara Otunnu, the LTTE leaders undertook to observe the provisions of the UN Convention on the Rights of the Child and to refrain from recruiting children or engaging them in combat. They also agreed not to impede refugees to return to their home areas or to interfere with humanitarian aid (Sri Lanka Monitor, May 1998: 4).

Advocacy Strategies

The agencies have employed two main types of advocacy strategies. The first strategy is lobbying of the combatants in Sri Lanka. The second strategy is lobbying of international actors who presumably can apply pressure on the combatants.

The first strategy, lobbying of the combatants, can be divided into three approaches. Firstly, 'protection by presence' is based on the idea that the presence of international field staff has a restraining influence on the combatants. It is built on the assumption that the presence of agencies will deter violations of human rights and humanitarian law by the combatants because agencies will potentially act as an agent for people whose rights have been violated. The Open Relief Centres run by UNHCR in Mannar and Pesalai are the most well known examples of this strategy. However, as its limitations became apparent, most notably during the war in the former Yugoslavia (Safe Heavens), but also in Sri Lanka, the concept has increasingly been questioned. The second approach is direct lobbying of the government and of the LTTE leadership. Agencies have lobbied the government to allow food supplies to areas under LTTE control and on several occasions the agency interventions have been successful.

Agencies have also raised issues regarding forceful resettlement and have been able to prevent this from happening. In relation to the LTTE, UNHCR has experienced two failed attempts at lobbying the LTTE into accepting organised return of displaced people to Jaffna. A third approach to advocacy is lobbying based on reports produced by the agencies themselves.

This is a strategy which has been used by Oxfam, SCF and Redd Barna. Both SCF and Redd Barna have commissioned a range of studies about key aspects of the situation of children in Sri Lanka, incorporating input from children themselves. The quote below exemplifies how SCF has tried to carve out a new role for itself through this process of gaining new knowledge about the situation of children: So much of the work that we have done over the past couple of years, although small, it has been able to better inform us as to the things that come with the long term effects of the conflict.

So we are positioning ourselves to be authoritative perhaps, to try and pressurise people to try and take something other than a short term approach to everything, and hence our interest in education comes from work that started with this, what we talked to communities about, what was important to them: water, shelter, pots and pans did not come on top of the list. It was consistently education. Families whose children have known nothing but the conflict were thinking about the future of their children rather then the next night in the shelter. So we tried to consistently produce material that reflect what people are thinking.

In addition to general reporting on the rights of children, both organisations also report in relation to the Child Rights Convention. This reporting takes place through the Consortium of Humanitarian Agencies based in Colombo and the Child Rights Group within the Consortium. The objective of this reporting is not only to assess the government's performance, but it is also to build knowledge which can provide a basis for further action by both NGOs and the government.

The quote below explains the importance of the Child Rights Convention to the advocacy work of these agencies: It provides us with backing. I think the Convention is the most useful tool that we have. When so many countries have signed up, they are accountable in a way. We are justified in telling a government: you have signed the convention and the report is due by Christmas. What kind of assistance do you need in order to finalise the report? We have helped writing many reports complementing government reports and we have also helped governments produce reports when they have had insufficient capacity.

In most cases, the agencies do not go public with their information but prefer to work informally. Only the ICRC has developed relatively clear guidelines as to when they should go public. According to the guidelines, the ICRC must have been a direct witness to ensure absolute certainty about the facts which are being reported, a breach of humanitarian law must have taken place, it must be serious, it must be repeated, and the intervention must not affect the victims.5 However, the ICRC's main criteria seem to be whether speaking up will help the victims concerned (Sommaruga 1997: 7, Sandoz 1992: 225). One aspect of this is an assessment of the risk that the ICRC will be denied access to the victims, in serious cases thrown out of the country, leaving the victims even more vulnerable than before.

When the Sri Lankan army bombed Navaly church in the Jaffna-peninsula on July 9, 1995 resulting in the deaths of over one hundred people6, the ICRC went out publicly with a carefully worded statement which not directly mentioned either the government nor the LTTE. It expressed its concern 'by the series of violent acts that have claimed innocent victims' and called upon the parties 'to respect civilian lives, property and places of refuge' (ICRC 1995). The government countered both by disputing the facts, arguing that it was not a direct hit on the church, but in the churchyard, and by fuelling a harsh press campaign against the ICRC. The ICRC-government relationship became strained for months and the ICRC had a difficult time operating.

Like the ICRC, other agencies have faced severe obstacles from the government when attempting to implement an advocacy mandate. These constraints have mainly taken two forms. One has been direct government interventions with agencies whereby the government has told agencies that it disapproves of their activities. The other has been statements by government spokespersons in the media which dispute the facts of a matter as they have been presented by the agencies. The responses of the government have subtly challenged the reliability of agency information and the legitimacy of their actions. These confrontations between the government and the agencies have resulted in periods of strained relations between them. The implicit threat which the agencies have faced is that the government would deny them access to displaced people in the Vanni or that it would deny them permits to work altogether. Therefore, it seems that the agencies have been reluctant to place themselves in a position in which they have had to confront the government. The second advocacy strategy seems to be the one favoured by NGOs: to provide information to and to lobby more powerful actors.

This strategy could be called 'leverage politics'.7 As one respondent put it: At the same time I think one of our tasks is to make available objective information. We have international staff there, of course most of the information comes from local staff which can be verified within limits. Information then is made available to the international community, so a lot of this information comes from us. Without us being directly involved. It is up to the politicians to decide on action. Both sides are really looking for the support of the people and they are both interested to be seen as adhering to basic international standards.

The agencies have regularly briefed their own embassies in Sri Lanka as well as their foreign ministries at home about the situation in the conflict areas. Forut and Redd Barna have been members of the London based NGO Forum on Sri Lanka which is an advocacy group for NGOs, both national and international, working in Sri Lanka. Oxfam developed a strategy for passing on information about humanitarian and human rights issues to more powerful players, such as the UN, the EU and donors.

The main arenas for international advocacy related to the conflict have been the UN Human Rights Commission, the UN Sub-Commission on Prevention of Discrimination and Protection of Minorities and the annual meeting of the major donors to the Sri Lankan government in Paris. The UN Human Rights Commission first passed a resolution on Sri Lanka in 1987 in which it asked the government to allow the ICRC to offer its services in Sri Lanka.

The UN Subcommission on Prevention of Discrimination and Protection of Minorities adopted a resolution on Sri Lanka in 1984 (Whall 1995: 323). NGOs have raised both peace and human rights issues on these occasions. They have urged the parties to find a peaceful resolution to the conflict, as well as trying to make donors make their aid programs conditional on the human rights performance of the Sri Lankan government.

MAKING IT WORK

According to Keck and Sikkink (1998) advocacy work requires a clear cognitive frame within which an issue can be defined and explained to a target audience. A cognitive frame serves to show that a given state of affairs can be changed through identifying the responsible parties and suggesting credible solutions. If one looks at advocacy issues which have been projected by the humanitarian agencies in Sri Lanka, they fall into three categories:

(i) humanitarian issues connected to the delivery of assistance to war affected people

(ii) human rights issues like forceful resettlement, disappearances and problems related to birth certificates and documentation

(iii) issues which are associated with the peace question.

Keck and Sikkink (1998) argue that an actor who is vulnerable is more likely to respond to advocacy pressure. They discuss vulnerability as a result of aid dependency as the most common type of vulnerability. The Sri Lankan government has to a certain degree been vulnerable in this respect and the annual donor meeting in Paris has provided a focus for NGO advocacy. However, by far the largest two donors, Japan and the Asian Development Bank, have not been targeted. When it comes to the potential for applying leverage and accountability vis à vis the LTTE this is much more limited. Being a largely self reliant guerrilla group, raising funding through taxation and trade, the LTTE is not dependent on any large donors which are accessible to advocacy pressure.

As for accountability politics, only states are signatories to human rights law while humanitarian law is binding both for states and for non-state actors. LTTE is, therefore, bound by humanitarian law and it has publicly stated that it will abide by humanitarian law. However, in practice, LTTE argues that humanitarian concerns are secondary to military imperatives, and that the group has limited resources to spend on ensuring that humanitarian law is upheld.8 On the other hand, the Sri Lankan army has a hierarchical structure whose top and intermediary leadership is accessible to advocacy efforts and whose rank and file can be brought together for training. LTTE has a much smaller number of mid-level officers, its rank and file is much less accessible and the leader, Prabakaran, has only been seen once by the ICRC, and not at all by representatives of the NGOs.10 Amnesty International and Human Rights Watch have drawn attention to human rights abuses by the LTTE and one of their sources is NGOs operating in these areas (Amnesty International 1996, Human Rights Watch/Asia 1995). So, although the LTTE is not formally accountable in relation to human rights law, as far as the LTTE is concerned with its image and international position it is presumably vulnerable to human rights criticisms.

Based on the discussion above it is possible to deduct that an optimal situation for successful advocacy would be a situation characterised by an issue which is humanitarian in character, a cognitive frame consisting of an international convention and a compatible, national belief system, a target which is integrated into the international community to allow for leverage politics to be employed, and possibly sanctions to be imposed, and a target which has made commitments either to international legal instruments or to national law. If one compares the Sri Lankan government and the LTTE on these characteristics, it becomes evident that an advocacy strategy vis à vis the government is more likely to succeed than an advocacy strategy vis à vis the

LTTE. This is because the government has signed up to binding international, legal instruments.

The government is integrated into the international community of states. As a recipient of aid, the government is also vulnerable to pressure from donor governments and organisations. In 1997 and 1998, the United Kingdom was the fourth largest donor of development aid to Sri Lanka, providing US$16 million. Norway was the fifth largest donor, providing US$15 million.10 Sri Lanka received a total of US$ 329 million in official development assistance in 1997 and US$ 490 million in 1998 (OECD 2000). As a guerrilla organisation, the LTTE is only committed to limited sections of international humanitarian law and there is little scope for leverage politics as LTTE is not dependent on funding from any governments or international organisations.

Neutrality: a Barrier to Advocacy?

The reason which is often given against taking up advocacy work, is that advocacy is not compatible with maintaining a neutral position. The argument is that advocacy could be perceived as taking sides or engaging in controversy. One of the organisations in the study put it in the following terms: ...very sensitive ground because you never get it right. The Sri Lankan government will say you are siding with the Tamils, the Tamils will say you are siding with the government.

The findings from Sri Lanka do not support the idea that neutrality is on the retreat. Rather all of the agencies emphasise their desire to remain neutral based on an operational definition of neutrality. Neutrality is seen as an instrument to achieve delivery of assistance within an environment which at times is perceived as hostile. The efforts which agencies make to balance their relationships to the combatants, in such a way that they are not perceived to be taking sides in the conflict, reflect this understanding of the concept of neutrality. While holding on to the concept of neutrality, agencies have explored avenues for advocacy. Firstly, the basis for their advocacy work has been their mandates which reflect international laws and conventions, or it has been the particular knowledge which they have gained through their access to the conflict areas. Secondly, their advocacy has been strictly linked to the consequences that the actions of the combatants have for their beneficiaries. Thirdly, the agencies also keep a low profile and they tend to 'decouple' advocacy work from their service delivery work. These strategies have worked in terms of maintaining neutrality in the sense that the agencies in general have been able to continue their service delivery work in the conflict areas.

MSF and ICRC are the strongest exponents of the strategies of using their mandates and knowledge obtained through their work in conflict areas as a way of combining advocacy and service delivery work. I briefly discussed ICRC above. The MSF model is to make advocacy an integral part of service delivery work. On the relationship between advocacy and service delivery, the MSF view is that advocacy is an integral part of service delivery: Advocacy is an integral part of our humanitarian mission. Therefore we do not talk about populations in need. We prefer to describe them as populations in danger. The concept of danger indicates that people should be protected against violence and human rights abuses. If they are not, then aid can easily be part of the repressive policies that have caused this suffering in the first place. Aid agencies have to be aware of the permanent danger of becoming government sub-contractors (Milliano 1996: 13).

In implementing its mandate in Sri Lanka, MSF Sri Lanka states that: 'We say what we are doing and what we are seeing'. When MSF witnessed violations of humanitarian law in, for example in September 1995 and July 1997, the organisation publicised the violations through press releases. MSF reporting vis à vis humanitarian law is based on medical evidence collected by MSF field staff and lobbying carried out by MSF is also based on medical evidence. As for human rights issues, MSF hands information on to the ICRC. MSF emphasises the need for absolute transparency vis à vis the combatants. In other words, MSF keeps the combatants informed about their work while also making public instances of violations of humanitarian law committed by the combatants. MSF has developed the concept of 'active impartiality' to describe advocacy work (Slim 1997b). Equally important is MSF's emphasis on transparency in relation to the combatants as a way of ensuring that they are perceived as neutral. The MSF approach to combining service delivery and advocacy was awarded the Nobel Peace Prize in 1999, as the Nobel Committee acknowledged the merits of combining service delivery work with advocacy.

What then are the policy implications for other NGOs of the approaches of the MSF and ICRC? Through a combination of transparency, and of basing their advocacy work on medical evidence, MSF manages to achieve its dual objectives of service delivery and advocacy. ICRC's advocacy work is based on humanitarian law and observance of the organisation's rules for when and how advocacy should be carried out. The best measure of the ability of these two organisations to remain neutral in the eyes of the combatants is probably their continued work in Sri Lanka for over ten years. In other words, based on carefully developed principles and balanced in relation to all parties to the conflict, advocacy and service delivery have been combined in the field. Could this model be adopted by NGOs and the UNHCR as well? MSF and ICRC provide services which may be considered of a more urgent nature than some services provided by NGOs. MSF and ICRC have a strong focus on medical services which may be seen by the combatants as less dispensable than, for example, income generating projects. The government may therefore tolerate more in terms of advocacy from these two organisations than from smaller NGOs. However, what NGOs and the UNHCR can learn from these two models is that an advocacy policy has to be carefully designed and planned by the organisation and potentially negative consequences for the organisation have to be assessed.

ORGANISATIONAL ISSUES

When agencies take up advocacy they become vulnerable to criticism from the combatants. The agencies in Sri Lanka have applied a range of responses to minimise their vulnerability. Organisational responses: knowledge, 'decoupling', alliances and transparency Advocacy is inherently political work. Keck and Sikkink (1998) use the word advocacy politics and talk about different types of advocacy politics.

When the organisation which is doing advocacy and the advocacy target have different goals, advocacy may lead to conflict between the two. Therefore, an organisation which is doing advocacy work often finds that its relationship to the environment is very different from an organisation which is doing service delivery work. What are the implications for organisational structure and behaviour of these different types of relationships to the environment?

Firstly, when organisations take up advocacy work, one component of this work is information politics as discussed by Keck and Sikkink (1998). The need for organisations to collect reliable information leads them to emphasise knowledge and knowledge creation as an important aspect of their work. Sometimes this approach is based on an acknowledgement that the organisation does not in fact know much about its beneficiaries. Developing a knowledge based organisation involves collecting information about relevant issues, and how they can be defined, within the local context as well as taking on new staff or training existing staff.

Building a knowledge based organisation may happen within the framework of an already existing structure, or it may involve radical changes in structure. The latter approach was developed by Redd Barna and, to some extent SCF, when their organisational policies changed to a focus on children's rights and large service delivery oriented programmes were abandoned.

Secondly, several of the organisations have 'decoupled' advocacy work from service delivery work. This is the model which is most widely prescribed in the literature as a means of managing pressure from the environment (Meyer and Scott 1992, Brunsson 1988, Elsbach and Sutton 1992).

According to this model, only very limited and discreet advocacy work is carried out in the country of conflict, and a more active role is played by the organisation abroad. The advocacy work carried out abroad could be either on specific issues related to the conflict in Sri Lanka, as has been the case with advocacy work carried out by Oxfam and Forut, or it could be on more general issues as has been the case with the advocacy work carried out by the ICRC.

However, Forut's experience has demonstrated that the strategy of carrying out advocacy abroad does not work in terms of avoiding controversy if information about the advocacy work abroad is fed into the country of conflict and ends up in the public domain.

Thirdly, I have argued that transparency is a strategy which is used by all of the agencies to maintain a constructive relationship with the combatants. As a staff member of MSF in Sri Lanka said: 'We say what we are doing and what we are seeing.' In addition to regular meetings and reporting to the combatants, which are activities that all the agencies carry out, Red Cross has taken transparency a step further by publishing its own newsletter in Sri Lanka, as well as explaining its work in the national newspapers to reach a broader constituency.

The emphasis which the agencies place on transparency, provision of information and dialogue with the combatants, is surprising in the context of organisational theory. Pfeffer and Salancik have argued that: ... organisations attempt to avoid influence and constraint by restricting the flow of information about them and their activities, denying the legitimacy of demands made upon them, diversifying their dependencies, and manipulating information to increase their own legitimacy (Pfeffer and Salancik 1978: 261).

The organisations in this study provide the combatants with information about their activities for at least three reasons.

Firstly, to pre-empt allegations that they are not impartial and neutral.

Secondly, to use as a defence in case they are accused of inappropriate activities and, thirdly, to build legitimacy for their work.

So, contrary to Pfeffer and Salancik's argument, organisations under pressure supply information about themselves and their activities to key actors rather than restricting it. Providing information serves the purposes of projecting and protecting the image of the organisation. By continually providing information, agencies attempt to persuade other actors that the activity is proper and that the organisation is a valid practitioner. These are the two elements which Suchmann (1995) defines as part of a strategy to build legitimacy.

Institutional theory suggests that gaining legitimacy from the environment is a key organisational concern which may impact both on organisational structure and action. Fourthly, foreign humanitarian agencies are susceptible to criticism exactly because they are foreign and primarily accountable to Western donors and their home constituencies.

One lesson which is reflected in much writing about advocacy work is the need for alliances with parties both inside and outside the NGO sector. Alliances may be with the business sector, churches or trade unions (Hall 1992, Covey 1995).

This idea may be particularly pertinent to foreign humanitarian agencies. In the Sri Lankan context, the importance of alliances between civil society and sensitive agents inside the establishment has been pointed out (Weerakoon 1997). The NGOs working in Sri Lanka have until recently not entered into alliances with organisations outside the NGO sector. However, this is changing with Redd Barna's and Save the Children's advocacy work.

They are developing relationships with civil society institutions, such as research institutions and advocacy groups on children's rights. One pronounced aim of this policy is to give legitimacy to the advocacy work that is carried out on child rights issues.

Oxfam, Forut and SCF have adopted the strategy of trying to link up with the views of their beneficiaries through different processes whereby the views of their beneficiaries are sought. However, the agencies have not taken the next logical step which would be to change their policies so that they would become more compatible with the views of their beneficiaries. UNHCR, Forut and SCF are the organisations which have most explicitly decided to work with the government in particular areas, either out of necessity or based on the idea of scaling up. All these strategies are based on a need to strengthen links between agencies and their environment so that they can become more effective and also increase their legitimacy.

CONCLUDING REMARKS

As organisations move from service delivery to advocacy the potential for confrontation with the combatants increases. Similarly, as organisations move from humanitarian aid and towards rehabilitation, human rights and peace, goals become less overlapping and the potential for confrontation increases. Moving in this direction increases the potential for conflict.

However, if human rights and peace work is implemented as services, such as training programmes, the potential for conflict becomes less. This is an approach which has been adopted widely by, for example, the ICRC which has implemented extensive training programmes for the Sri Lankan army on humanitarian law. As agencies move towards the right in Table 3 to a situation where human rights and peace issues become more prominent on the agenda, the potential for confrontation with the combatants increases. Similarly, as their role changes from service delivery to advocacy this change also increases the potential for confrontation. For example, activities which fall within box A, service delivery of humanitarian aid, are less controversial then activities within box H: advocacy on the peace issue.

This combination makes peace issues hard to tackle for foreign NGOs. The agencies in Sri Lanka have developed a range of organisational responses to manage the tensions between service delivery and advocacy. They include building a knowledge based organisation, decoupling, transparency and alliance building. What are the lessons which the international NGO community can draw from these discussions?

First of all, the experience from Sri Lanka demonstrates that it is possible to combine advocacy with neutrality, although it requires a fine balancing act from the agencies. Strong forces are pushing relief NGOs in the direction of advocacy, most notably a demand from their Southern counterparts and even from their beneficiaries.

Secondly, combining advocacy and service delivery constitutes an organisational challenge which the agencies have to tackle. In addition to the challenges which have been listed above, the question of the qualifications and training of agency staff is important.

More research is needed on the advocacy strategies of humanitarian agencies in complex political emergencies. One possible design could trace advocacy efforts from the local and national level and through to the international level using a multilevel, possibly comparative, approach.

4

THE LIMITATIONS OF NGOs

Based on case studies of NGOs in three cities, this paper discusses some of the common constraints on the ability of Chinese social welfare NGOs to perform both service delivery and advocacy functions at the present time. It shows that the effectiveness of NGOs is above all conditioned by their institutional environment. When the general level of social welfare provision in a country is low, it also sets a limit to what NGOs can achieve. Given the crucial importance of the institutional context to NGO performance, the paper concludes by arguing that unless the context is changed, NGO performance is unlikely to be drastically improved by capacity building programmes that only focus on these organisations themselves.

INTRODUCTION

With the future direction of administrative reform captured in the slogan 'small government, big society' and the development of the social welfare system guided by the principle of 'socialising social welfare', it has become fashionable to talk about the potentials of NGOs in delivering social welfare in both government and academic circles in China. Although there has been no shortage of speeches and articles setting out in somewhat grand terms the multiple functions which NGOs can perform, very few empirical studies have been carried out to see whether those high hopes can be realised in the current institutional setting and to find out what constraints are faced by NGOs in assuming a more significant role in a plural social welfare system.

This paper attempts to address some of the constraints on the ability of Chinese social welfare NGOs to perform both service delivery and advocacy functions at present. It is mostly based on case studies of NGOs in Guangzhou, Beijing, and Shanghai that provide services to disabled children and their parents, but I have also drawn on my knowledge of organisations in other fields and localities. Researchers on Chinese NGOs often make careful distinctions between organisations with different degrees of autonomy and voluntariness. The mass and semi-official organisations are often created top-down and their main task is to perform various functions on behalf of the state. The popular organisations, on the other hand, are born of private initiatives and exist primarily to respond to society's needs or to represent its interests in a bottom-up fashion. The case studies for this paper consist mainly of popular organisations. The various constraints on these NGOs' ability to serve the interests of their clients or members therefore highlight the current limit to popular participation in achieving better welfare for vulnerable groups in China.

The Context for the Development of Social Welfare NGOs

This section briefly discusses some contextual factors which directly affect the ability of Chinese NGOs to deliver social services and advocate for enhanced welfare provision for their constituencies. The Chinese welfare system for vulnerable and marginalised members of society is a residual system. The state only assumes direct responsibility when other institutional arrangements have failed. Even then, the provision tends to be narrow and minimal. To give just one example, according to the 1987 nation-wide sample survey of disabled people, 99.85% of disabled children in China were supported by families or relatives, only 0.15% lived on financial support from the state or collectives (Wang and Wang, 1992:55-59).

Despite rapid development in recent years, there is still a conspicuous shortage of social services for various groups with special needs. In some areas, service remains non-existent. In 1987, only 55.2% of disabled children aged between 6 and 14 in China attended school, which accounted for 61.6% of the total number of disabled children who were judged to be able to attend school (ibid:133). When the famous Zhiling School, the first private school for mentally disabled children in mainland China, was founded in Guangzhou in 1985, there was not a single school, whether government-run or private, for such children in this city with a population of nearly seven million. Neither was the option of integrated education in normal schools available to mentally disabled children. Up to 1992, official statistics showed that only 18.13% of children with sight-related, hearing and speech-related, or mental disabilities in Guangzhou were able to attend school (Yao, 1999).

Many areas of social services are marked by the scant supply of specialists and professionally trained personnel. A good example is service for autistic children. An analysis of 500 cases from all over the country revealed that less than 2% of autistic children in China were diagnosed before the age of three, which means the loss of precious opportunities of early training and rehabilitation for many autistic children. Furthermore, many hospitals have no specialists who are able to diagnose autism, therefore about 95% of autistic children were only diagnosed after the parents had taken them to many different hospitals, often in many different cities. Since there are no specialised agencies which can provide professional advice, counselling, and training for parents of autistic children in most Chinese cities, even after their children are correctly diagnosed, many parents are unable to help the children to improve their condition. Very few autistic children are able to attend school. Even in special education schools for mentally disabled children, few teachers have been trained to teach autistic children (Tian, 1999).

One direction in which the socialisation of social welfare has proceeded is to open up state welfare institutions, which used to admit only people with no alternative means of support, such as elderly people with neither income nor families to rely on, to self-financed clients. State welfare homes tend to be much less cost-effective than private welfare homes, However, since state welfare homes are still heavily subsidised by the government, they are able to charge less from self-financing clients than private welfare homes, which results in unfair competition with non-government institutions.

Another government strategy for socialising social welfare is to encourage all kinds of private investment in social services, whether profit-oriented or not. Consequently non-profit organisations have also had to compete with for-profit ones, some of which pay no regard to the quality of service but are able to charge less fees by using lower-grade facilities and hiring fewer staff, hence attracting some low-income clients. The existence of such institutions also puts pressure on NGOs which try to maintain certain basic standards.

Although these problems have been noted by government policy makers and some efforts are being made to address them, they are unlikely to disappear in the near future. Even assuming that further reform does not involve such difficult tasks as balancing conflicting goals and challenging vested interests, to improve the environment for NGOs the government will need at least to put in a new set of regulations on such issues as quality control and financial supervision and to develop the capacity to enforce them, which will take time to happen.

The traditional work unit based social security arrangement for the urban population saw a wide range of benefits, including pension, health care and housing, being offered exclusively to public-sector employees. Reform is currently underway to install a new system which extends social insurance coverage to people employed outside the public sector, but it is still at an early stage. Whereas private sector employers who are able to offer salaries several times higher than those offered by the public sector may be able to compete with the latter to some extent in recruiting skilled or talented people, NGOs are clearly in no position to join the competition at the moment.

Current Government Policies Regarding NGOs

All would-be NGOs are required to find a 'professional management unit' to act as their sponsoring agency first. Only after obtaining the approval of their sponsors can NGOs apply for registration with Civil Affairs Departments, which is mandatory. The sponsor must be an official agency above the county level or an organisation authorised by such an agency. It must also be 'relevant' to the activities proposed by the NGO, i.e., it must have responsibilities in the same field in which the NGO operates. Current regulations also stipulate that only one NGO of each kind may register at each administrative level. For example, if there is already an association of physically disabled people in Beijing, no new association of this kind will be allowed to register.

Although individual NGOs may have received subsidies, allocations, or donations from various government agencies on an ad hoc basis, there is not yet any institutionalised funding for NGOs from the government.

Private Philanthropy

The field of philanthropic activities has been dominated by state-backed funds or fundraising drives. The former include the China Youth Development Foundation (which runs the internationally well-known Project Hope), the China Charities Federation, and various provincial and municipal charity foundations, while a typical example of the latter is the nation-wide fundraising campaign after the flood in 1998. Since the state-backed initiatives are able to use all kinds of state-controlled resources and even official organisational systems to mobilise private donations, for example, by organising semi-compulsory donations through work units, they have considerably squeezed the charitable resources for NGOs.

Corporate rather than individual donations currently constitute the bulk of charitable giving. Various evidence suggests that corporate donors prefer to give their money to large state-backed funds instead of small NGOs. The reason is best summarised by the authors of a book on the fundraising strategies of the China Youth Development Foundation (CYDF): Businesses consider donations to CYDF a form of advertising which tends to be cheaper and more effective than commercial advertising. In the words of a CYDF staff member: 'Our fundraising department has become an advertising agency.' (Sun et al, 1999:162). CYDF offers various publicity opportunities to corporate donors.

A main task of its fundraising department is to organise donation ceremonies for its donors which are attended by top state officials and ensured coverage by major news media. This service has become so standardised that all a corporate donor needs to do is to sign a detailed agreement with CYDF which specifies the amount it is going to donate.

Depending on the amount, CYDP promises to secure the presence of state officials of a certain rank at the ceremony and coverage of the event by a certain number of media units. Once an agreement has been signed, the corporate donor can leave everything to CYDP and just wait to hand over the cheque and have its representative shaking hands with state leaders in front of media cameras at the ceremony (ibid). Given what state-backed funds can offer corporate donors, it is not surprising that they appear to be far more attractive targets of charitable donations than pure NGOs.

Do the state-backed funds share the money they raise with NGOs? Although some NGOs have received funding from organisations such as the China Charities Federation, the practice, like government funding for NGOs, is not institutionalised. Furthermore, the majority of the funds raised by the state-backed funds are spent by themselves, which mostly go to projects not easily distinguishable from government activities and are usually implemented by the government.

Political Culture and Modes of Popular Participation

The political institutions of a country shape the way its people participate in politics. It has been noted that in many aspects the political institutions in China favour individualised action over collective action. Whereas the institutional arrangements in many societies make it difficult for ordinary citizens to influence policies at the implementation stage, hence forcing them to pursue their interests by targeting the agenda setting or policy formulation stages of the policy process, the institutional design in China is such that the reverse is true. In China, policies are usually not formulated in a precise form and bureaucrats tend to have considerable leeway in interpreting and implementing policies according to local situations. As a result, it is much easier for citizens to pursue their interests by influencing policy implementation, which, compared to influencing agenda setting and policy formulation, puts less demand on group-based activities (Shi, 1997).

Collective actions are obviously not helped by the government's attitude, either. On the one hand, the government sends out clear messages that it does not like autonomous collective actions; on the other hand, it has defined the 'proper organisational channels' for citizens to pursue their legitimate private interests and encourages people to use these channels. Research finds that the officially sanctioned methods of interest articulation have been very successful in channelling people's participation and they have served to discourage collective actions and confrontational strategies (ibid).

In addition, the institutional design in China made the work unit the key institution in the distribution of resources. The state controlled most of the goods and services crucial to the daily lives of its citizens. These were allocated to work units and then distributed within them. People's primary strategy for pursuing their interests therefore involved competing with their colleagues in the same work unit for a larger share of a fixed amount of resources. This further thwarted group formation and group-based activities (ibid). Although market reform has significantly reduced people's dependence on their work units, the influence of the work unit system on the culture of participation may still linger.

Finally, as mentioned above, lower-echelon bureaucrats in China are given much discretionary power in implementing policies. Such an arrangement induces ordinary citizens to focus their energy on influencing individual officials rather than the policy-making process. This in turn encourages participants to pursue such strategies as developing patron-client ties with officials or using guanxi (personal connections) to get what they want, which may be more cost-effective than other strategies, e.g., engaging in confrontational political actions to pressure officials to meet their demands.

NGOs and Service Delivery

Owing to the lack of stable funding from either government or private sources, most NGOs I studied have to charge for their services. Needlessly to say, this results in people who need the service but cannot afford it being excluded. Given that the government currently does not provide any subsidy for people with special needs, e.g. disabled people, even those who are able to pay for some services cannot afford high prices. As a result, most NGOs set the standard of their services at a very modest level in order to make them affordable to the average client. Since both the quality and range of services currently provided by fee-charging NGOs tend to be determined primarily by how much the average user in China is able to pay, the ability of these organisations to experiment with new ideas and develop innovative service models is seriously limited.

The same is also true of NGOs which do not charge fees but rely entirely on donations. Unless they have stable and abundant sources of funding, the amount of donations they raise is unlikely to support high-quality services. An illuminating example is a private orphanage in Wuhan which experimented with a new model of care. Before starting the orphanage, the founder visited both state-run children's welfare homes and SOS children's villages set up in China by the charity SOS-Kinderdorf International.

The former were large institutions which deprived orphans of experience of normal family life. Although the latter are organised around small group homes, they only employ single women as house mothers, so the experience of family life they offer children is not entirely normal, either. In order to provide a better alternative for orphans, the founder of the Wuhan orphanage organised it into small group homes and recruited married couples to work as carers. Each couple was assigned a few orphans who came to live with them and their own children. The experiment failed because the modest allowance for each orphan which the orphanage was able to provide could only support a relatively frugal life. If their own children were to be treated in the same way as the orphans living with them, which was essential to the success of this care model, it would mean a considerable decrease in the living standard of their own children, which proved to be too difficult for the house parents to accept. After some time, the founder had to abandon the experiment and reorganised the orphanage along the line of state-run children's welfare homes, which seemed to be the cheapest way to care for a sizable number of children.

While NGO accountability to their clients may be weak where the service is free, with fee-charging NGOs one would normally expect the clients to be in some position to demand that the service be delivered to their satisfaction. This does not seem to be the case at the moment. The reason is simple: as mentioned earlier, specialised social service agencies are currently in very short supply. At places where one or two do exist, they are the only choices. To some people, any service is better than no service at all. The case of one family in Shanghai with an autistic child can serve to illustrate this situation. The mother of the child divorced her husband and abandoned the child. The father therefore has to care for the child on his own. He has a salary of around 1,400 yuan per month. The minimum living standard in Shanghai is currently set at around 300 yuan per person per month, which means this man is not qualified for financial assistance from the government.

The man needs to work full-time in order to earn the salary to support himself and his son. Since it is too difficult to look after an autistic child all by himself while working full-time, he tried to find a residential home for the child. There are very few residential homes for mentally disabled children in Shanghai. He learned about a private home which was said to be good, but it charged over 1,000 yuan a month-obviously beyond the means of this man. With considerable efforts he finally obtained a place for his son in a private non-profit home whose price was affordable to him. However, its service was not very good and after some time the child's condition worsened. During my research I also interviewed a friend of this man who had visited the child at the residential home.

She was shocked by its poor quality of care and wanted to make complaints to the management of the residential home. However, the father begged her not to do so. Even though it was far from ideal, obtaining a place in that home for his son had not been easy since it had a long waiting list. Besides, he had no other place to go. This case is not unique. In other cities, I also encountered similar situations in which parents did not dare to complain about the services because they had no other option and they thought complaining might result in their children being discriminated against in the future.

In fact, in some places a perverse situation seems to have developed: instead of witnessing clients pushing NGOs to improve their services, one finds NGO managers criticising clients for obstructing their attempts to upgrade the services or hiring better-qualified staff. The comments of a veteran NGO leader in the field of service for mentally disabled children in Guangzhou sum up the situation very well:

Since private social services in mainland China do not receive funding from the government, the primary consideration of parents is the affordability of the services, not children's needs, which have not been put in the first place. In Hong Kong, parents play the role of spokesperson for the users of social services. They monitor the performance of service agencies, but Guangzhou parents do not wish to play the role of watchdogs, because if they ask for better services, the cost will also rise (which will be born by themselves), so they don't raise such issues, and there can be no breakthrough in terms of user participation.

Under present circumstances, where several service providers co-exist in one locality, instead of creating pressure on every provider to offer better service to users, the competition between them may actually be played out to the detriment of users' interest. This seems to be what happened in Guangzhou with regard to residential care service for mentally disabled people. The service was started by two NGOs. Later, when the 'socialisation of social welfare' policy encouraged private investment in social services, a couple of for-profit organisations were also set up. The investors were attracted to this field because apparently existing service could only accommodate a small proportion of the total need in Guangzhou, so they thought there was a big market out there to be occupied. What the investors of the for-profit organisations failed to realise was that many people who needed the service still could not afford it. The NGOs were charging between 580 and 750 yuan per month for service during weekdays. Another 240 to 400 yuan was charged for service on weekends. On top of that, parents also needed to pay any medical cost which might arise. In 1998, the per capita disposable income of Guangzhou residents was only 938 yuan per month (Guangzhou Yearbook, 1999), which means the fees charged by the NGOs were already quite high relative to the income of the average Guangzhou family.

Not surprisingly, the for-profit organisations had an extremely hard time finding enough clients, even though their prices were only slightly higher than those of the

NGOs. To attract clients, one for-profit organisation introduced a service called the lifelong care arrangement. The arrangement allows parents to pay a lump sum when they send their children to a residential home. The home then commits itself to take eare of the children for as long as they live. Some parents want this kind of service because they worry about what may happen to their children once they themselves pass away, given that these children cannot live on their own and there is no guarantee that they will be well provided for by the state. In effect, the lifelong care arrangement offers clients insurance against an uncertain future. However, the insurance came with strings attached, for the for-profit organisation would not refund parents once they had paid the lump sum. Even if parents were dissatisfied with the service later on they could not pull out, unless they were prepared to lose all the money they paid at the outset for lifelong care. In 1998, the lump sum charged by the for-profit organisation was 100,000 yuan, a huge amount of money to an ordinary Chinese family.

What about clients who chose not to join the lifelong care scheme but to pay the fees on a monthly basis? The for-profit organisation also made it difficult for them to quit by charging a 'sponsorship fee' when they first signed up for its service. The sponsorship fee, which was also non-refundable, was set at 30,000 yuan in 1998, again a huge amount which few families could afford to lose.

Obviously, the non-refundable charges seriously undermined users' rights of choice and exit and it allowed the service provider to keep its clients without offering good service, but the for-profit organisation succeeded in snatching away a few of the NGOs' clients with the lifelong care offer. Angered by such unfair competition, the NGO which was the main competitor of the for-profit organisation then decided to introduce non-refundable charges as well. Eventually this practice was also copied by other organisations. This case shows that when competition is still not well regulated, instead of increasing choices to users, it may actually curtail user choice, and the entry of for-profit organisations in a field of service dominated by NGOs may drag down rather than push up the standards of NGOs.

Because they cannot offer competitive salaries, let alone the kind of social security provisions which have largely remained the prerogative of public sector employees, NGOs are not able to attract many highly-trained or experienced people.

Most NGOs in big cities such as Beijing and Guangzhou hire migrants from rural areas or small cities in less developed regions, or laid-off workers, who need to be trained on the job. Inevitably this affects the quality of their services. In all the cities where I have conducted research, well-off families choose not to use NGO service because they are not satisfied with the qualification of their staff. The difficulty in finding people who are willing to commit themselves to an organisation which offers little security and no prospect of a high-flying career or big earnings also made many founders of NGOs hire relatives or friends to work for them when they first started. Later, when they expanded and hired more people on the market, strife often broke out between those staff who had special connections to the managers and those who did not. At least in some of the NGOs I studied, internal strife had seriously affected the moral of the staff, which in turn affected the performance of the organisations.

But the problem is not just NGOs' inability to offer attractive remuneration or career opportunities. As mentioned earlier, in many fields there are simply not enough professionally trained people. To use the example of service for mentally disabled children again, when the first NGO, the Zhiling School, was set up in Guangzhou to provide special education for these children, it was difficult to find any people trained in special education or care for mentally disabled children-hardly a surprise considering that there was not a single special education school in the city at the time. None of Zhiling's early staff had any previous training in working with mentally disabled children, but fortunately Zhiling's main donor in Hong Kong helped to train them.

Over the years, many specialists in Hong Kong were invited to give instructions to Zhiling staff. Hong Kong social work students also came to Zhiling for placement every year. Later, some Zhiling staff left to found another NGO called Huiling, which also provides education and care for mentally disabled children, as well as adults. Today, veteran Zhiling and Huiling staff are considered experts in the field of service for mentally disabled children, so much so that they have been asked by the provincial Disabled Persons' Federation to train special education teachers from other agencies.

When experienced employees are in short supply and they tend to be the veteran staff of the earliest organisations in a particular field, new comers in the field are often forced to 'steal' the staff of the existing organisations. In the places where more than one organisation exist in a single field, many old scores tend to have accumulated between the different organisations for taking away each other's staff, among other things. As one parent in Guangzhou remarked: 'There is a chasm between government and popular organisations, but there is also much animosity between the popular organisations.'

When organisations working on the same issues choose to 'grow old and die without having had any dealings with each other', as the Guangzhou parent put it, instead of working together, what implications does it have for their ability to advocate for the interests of their clients? This question leads me to the next section on NGO's efficacy in advocacy.

NGOS AND ADVOCACY

Not only do NGOs compete for each other's skilled staff, but they also compete for clients, funding, media attention, and favours parcelled out by government officials. This unfortunate situation does not augur well for NGO solidarity. In addition, the culture of participation in China also seems to work against NGO collective action. As explained earlier, the institutional design in China encourages individual actions aimed at persuading bureaucrats to use their discretionary power to the advantage of the parties engaging in those actions. At present the government has no clearly stipulated obligation to support NGOs, therefore they cannot demand any concrete assistance from the government by citing any regulation or policy. Meanwhile, a particular NGO can often obtain some individually negotiated favours from officials or government agencies if it enjoys good relationships with them or is skilled at soliciting their support. Consequently it makes more sense for individual NGOs to quietly cultivate good relationships with government officials in order to obtain particularistic favours than to work together with other NGOs to fight for universal rights and benefit. When a particular NGO has indeed received special favours from government officials, it is usually wise for it to keep it from other NGOs. Under such circumstances, the NGO is also likely to consider its own interests to be better served by forging close ties with the government rather than with other NGOs, and it is less likely to damage its good relations with the government by challenging any government policy or practice.

A few examples can serve to demonstrate this situation. A NGO in Guangzhou managed to get 100,000 yuan from a government fund in 1999. Its manager told some other NGOs about it. Afterwards she was reproached for being ungrateful by officials, who said: 'You should have kept quiet. Why did you have to let everybody know? What can we do if they all come here to ask for money?' In Beijing, grapevine rumours suggest that a couple of NGOs have powerful patrons in the relevant government agencies. Each of them is identified by other NGOs as the protege of a particular government official. Other NGOs all have bitter tales to tell about how the patrons treated them unfairly in order to give advantage to their proteges. One NGO manager went to ask an official, who was said to be an old friend of the manager of her rival organisation, why his agency had given four times more money to the other NGO, which she considered to be poorly managed. She was told that since her organisation was in a stronger position, more money should go to the weaker one.

When NGOs working in the same field feud with each other, it also hinders collective actions by their members or clients. A few years ago, a NGO leader in one of the cities where I have conducted research asked the parents of children who received service from her organisation to take the lead in forming a parents' association in order to promote the rights of mentally disabled people. The plan was to bring together all the parents of mentally disabled children in that city under the association. However, it was frustrated by the long-standing friction between the NGOs from the very beginning. As the president of the association told me:

If we call our organisation the association of parents of X city, then we cannot just have parents linked to one organisation. However, since the association was formed at the suggestion of the leader of one NGO, others all identified us with this particular NGO. This rather limited our scope, so we decided that in order to avoid being identified with this NGO we should adopt a detached attitude and place ourselves above the concerns of individual organisations. However, this attitude offended the NGO leader who first proposed the association so she also started to give us the cold shoulder. Since other people were not showing much interest in us and this NGO leader also cold-shouldered us, we were left in an increasingly awkward position. So, after organising a few activities we did not want to carry on any more.

Factionalism was not the only problem which had plagued the parents' association. Government policy on the registration of NGOs was another major obstacle it had encountered in striving to be an effective advocate for the interests of its members. Since the Disabled Persons' Federation, a semi-official organisation, already exists in every city, other organisations which aim to represent the interests of disabled people are unlikely to be allowed to register.

In any case, the parents' association could not persuade any government agency to agree to act as its sponsor, therefore it could not register itself and remained strictly speaking an illegal organisation.

Although the government did not take any action against it, its lack of a legitimate status further dampened the enthusiasm of its members. As the president said: 'Every time we want to organise a meeting or send out a notice to our members, we cannot just go ahead with it. We have to do it through the disabled person's federation. They said to us: 'You are illegal.' So there is a big unresolved problem there for us.'

In another city, some parents of autistic children organised regular activities amongst themselves for years. They called themselves a 'club' although it appeared to be a full-blown formal organisation in every respect. For example, the members elected an executive council once every four years and they paid annual membership fees which were used to publish a newsletter, among other things.

The club organised a wide range of activities, e.g., inviting specialists from other cities to give training and lectures to its members; conducting surveys of the needs of families with autistic children; drawing media attention to the lack of social service for autistic children. In fact, it was the best-organised grassroots autonomous organisation I had ever come across in China. Since 1996, the club had been trying to register as an independent organisation. Obviously it had not been easy for it to gain approval from the government. When representatives of the club first went to see government officials, they were considered troublemakers and were refused a reception. However, with perseverance and the right tactics the club eventually gained the sympathy of relevant government officials. In 1998, the Civil Affairs Bureau of the city finally decided to allow the club to register. However, before the registration went ahead, the Falun Gong incident took place. Afterwards the registration of new popular organisations was frozen and the club was told by civil affairs officials that no new organisation of its kind would be approved in the next 5 to 10 years.

With the campaign to straighten out social organisations underway after the Falun Gong incident, the members of the club were afraid of carrying on their activities without a legitimate status, therefore the club was left with one choice, i.e., to become the 'subsidiary' of a registered organisation. The city has a semi-official organisation called the Mental Health Association. Its leaders agreed to let the parents' club 'hang under' it. However, there were serious concerns among the parents that once the club became a subsidiary organisation of the Mental Health Association, it would lose its autonomy, and its freedom to organise activities would be restricted. The fear seemed to be well-founded. As one parent related to me:

Last time we met with the secretary general of the Association he said: 'In the past some parents insisted on remaining independent. They were going too far.' Then I mentioned that we wanted to invite certain experts from other cities to come here to give us some training. The secretary general immediately reacted by saying: 'Once you have joined our association, we will take care of these things. You parents can just sit back and act as our advisers.'

Members of the club split up into two camps: those who favoured affiliation with the Mental Health Association, because this seemed to be the only legitimate means for them to continue working for the interests of autistic children and their families; and those who were against affiliation with the association, thinking that they could only carry out effective advocacy by being an independent organisation. Eventually those parents who favoured affiliation with the association joined it as individual members of its newly-formed Youth and Children Branch. The rest of the parents, a minority, became 'dispersed', and the club ceased operation. The parents who joined the association had hoped that some of them would be allowed to serve on the executive council of the Youth and Children Branch, so that they would have some influence on its decision-making, but it turned out that the association did not reserve a single place on the council for them. When I spoke to a couple of the parents who joined the association four months afterwards, they remained disappointed about the benefit of the new arrangement.

The collapse of the parents' club shows how NGO's advocacy function can be seriously restricted by current government regulations, but there are also other factors which prevent bottom-up NGOs from becoming effective advocates for their members. One major obstacle seems to be the prevalent pessimism (or realism) among ordinary people about what they can achieve with their actions. In my interviews with parent leaders and NGO managers, many of them stressed that NGOs should not set unrealistic goals for themselves and should be sympathetic to the government's position. For example:

When so many able-bodied people have been laid off, how can we realistically expect the government to give subsidies to families with disabled people, or find disabled people jobs? My brother lives in New Zealand. I have heard from him that in New Zealand the government takes care of everything for disabled children. There are special provisions for them so they receive more benefits than normal children. If we want China to do the same, I am not even sure if it can be achieved 50 years from now, so I don't blame the government. There is no point in pressuring it to do what it is incapable of doing.

I have said on various occasions that the economy of our country has not developed to a stage when we can expect the government alone to pay for the care of our disabled children, so let individuals, families, and society all contribute to it. I always say to other parents that we should face the reality and should not shout abuses in public whenever we are dissatisfied with things.

Government officials are not really unsympathetic to our cause, so I have much understanding for them. For example, I ran into a retired director of the Education Bureau and he said to me: 'Don't blame me for refusing to support you in the past. We really did not have enough money. You should have seen the condition of normal schools. When normal schools were still seriously under-funded, where could we find the resources for special education schools?' So I said to him: 'Yes, I understand.'

Even if they are not totally pessimistic about their ability to make a difference, most people want quick solutions to their problems and are impatient to wait for advocacy activities to change government policies or popular attitudes. Most revealing is the remark of a participant at a group discussion during a national conference of parents of mentally disabled children. The remark was made in response to another participant's suggestion that they contact representatives to the People's Congress to ask them to introduce new legislation concerning social service provision for disabled children:

> It is too slow a remedy to be of any help. Even if we can make the People's Congress adopt new legislation to provide social services for disabled children, it may take five years for it to happen, but we cannot wait that long. By then our children will have become grown-ups. So let us focus on practical issues instead.

The scepticism about what can be achieved plus preoccupation with immediate needs make many people reluctant to devote time and energy to any activity which does not promise quick results or concrete benefit to themselves. This is another factor which explains why the association of parents of mentally disabled people mentioned above has not being an effective advocacy organisation. As the president said: 'The Chinese people are very practical. They only make investments when they are assured of returns. If there is going to be a 50% gain, people will give you 50% support, otherwise they give you nothing. Because there was no concrete benefit, parents were not keen on the association.'

In another case, a British couple, both specialists in education and rehabilitation for mentally disabled children, founded an organisation called Guangdong Special Children Parent Club in Guangzhou. The British couple obtained external funding to set up a resource centre for parents of mentally disabled children. The centre employs both administrative and professional staff. The latter provide professional consultation and assessment services for parents. The club's 100 or so members include parents of autistic children as well as parents of children with other types of mental disability, e.g., Down Syndrome and cerebral palsy. Although the club is intended to bring families in similar situations together so that they can join forces in 'improving public perceptions, awareness and attitudes toward children with disabilities', instead of pulling together, it seems that the members of the club have formed informal subgroups which quarrel with each other over the use of the club's resources.

The preoccupation with immediate needs as opposed to long-term goals drew parents of children with the same type of disability together. For example, parents of autistic children organised activities specifically targeting autism using the resources of the club. Other parents were disgruntled because they felt those families got more out of the public resources of the club than they did. Parents of autistic children remained unrepentant, saying that the resources of the club were for everybody, so if other parents did not know how to make good use of the resources it was their problem. Meanwhile they also started to organise activities amongst themselves outside the club to avoid squabbles with other parents, which further weakened the sense of unity among members of the club.

CONCLUSION

In this paper I have focused on some of the problems that prevent NGOs from acting as high-quality service providers and effective advocates for their constituencies. This is not to deny the positive contributions which NGOs have already made towards meeting the social welfare needs of vulnerable groups in society and raising general awareness of their conditions. Most of the problems mentioned here are actually not internal problems of NGOs, but external constraints that prevent NGOs from realising their full potentials.

Nevertheless, my case studies suggest that the strength of NGOs either as service providers or as advocates for disadvantaged people cannot be automatically assumed but must be empirically proved. The effectiveness of NGOs is inevitably conditioned by their institutional environment. In a country where the general level of social welfare provision is still very low and where private philanthropy is still underdeveloped, it may simply not be possible for NGOs to supply high quality social services in a sustainable way, at least not on any meaningful scale. In fact, it might be argued that NGOs should not even aim at providing its clients with a level of care and support that is beyond what is available to other members of the society, as it would prevent NGOs from gaining broad social support for their work.

I hope my case studies have also helped to show that most of the problems currently faced by Chinese NGOs have no quick or easy solutions. At the moment capacity building for Chinese NGOs is high on the agenda of many donor agencies. Partly as a result of donor interest, many organisations and individuals have been busy organising training programmes for Chinese NGOs. However, the problems afflicting these NGOs cannot simply be removed by, say, teaching them some fund-raising techniques, or telling them the importance of working together with other NGOs. The situation is far more complicated, and to help NGOs to assume more responsibility in the reforming social welfare system we may have to look beyond the NGOs themselves and direct our efforts at improving the general context for the development of these organisations.

5

SOCIAL CAPITAL IN BRITAIN

In an influential 1999 article on social capital in Britain, Peter Hall cites Britain as a counter-example to Robert Putnam's well-known analysis of declining social capital in the United States (Hall 1999). Hall claims that there has been no equivalent erosion of social participation in Britain, although there has been an apparent decline in social trust.

To explain this apparent paradox, Hall then proposes that the decline in trust may be due to changing values, as well as government policies and changes in social integration. Finally he argues that the British case provides broader lessons about distributional issues and the importance of government policy in influencing levels of social capital.

In this paper we draw in newly available data sets to update Hall's assessment of the levels of social capital in Britain and provide additional analysis. The data indicates that formal participation in voluntary organisations and political engagement are increasingly concentrated in the middle and upper middle classes.

In addition levels of generalised social trust have levelled out and remain low. We suggest that there are influences which were not fully considered by Hall, such as the rise in income inequality during the 1980s and the changing nature of working life. We argue that the distributional issues are critical to considering the overall levels of social capital in Britain, and that factors such as inequality , and class divisions are important societal factors when assessing social capital on a societal basis.

INTRODUCTION

Peter Hall's analysis of the state of social capital, 'social networks, both formal and informal' in Britain follows Robert Putnam's work suggesting that such networks are in decline in America. In particular, he is interested in 'the extent to which individuals have contact with others, beyond the sphere of the family or market, and notably the kind of face to face relations of relative equality associated with participation in common endeavours." (p418)

He begins by investigating indicators of formal social involvement: membership, volunteering and charitable giving, and concludes that the indicators present a picture of robust - even growing - formal involvement. He then examines informal sociability; available leisure time, and where it is spent, including pubs and sports clubs, and finds a pattern of increasing sociability. Hall attributes his assessment of social networks in Britain as being on the whole in quite good shape to three factors: significantly expanded access to higher education, a less rigidly stratified class structure, and government action supporting community involvement.

However, the figures for levels of generalised social trust in Britain do not appear to tell the same story, declining significantly from 44% to 30% between 1990 and 1995. Here Hall offers two possible explanations: a change in the moral climate of society away from collective concerns to far more individualistic ones, tied in part to the Thatcher government, and reflected in rising moral relativism. He also speculates that the nature of participation may be changing in ways not reflected in traditional indicators.

The concluding discussion explores the relationship of these patterns to democratic participation. Hall suggests that the generally high levels of voting support the view that political participation is widespread, which he believes further supports the view that social capital in Britain is strong. But he does raise concerns about the uneven distribution of participation among social classes, and about evidence of generational changes in attitudes to participation.

Hall's data showing robust levels of participation in formal voluntary activity coupled with declining social trust presents a paradox : how can the activities which are supposed to engender social networks and social capital be apparently maintaining their strength, while an important aspect of social capital, i.e. generalised social trust, is in decline?

This raises a more general conceptual confusion around causality in social capital, namely whether social capital contributes to the creation of generalised social trust, or whether social trust is an element of and contributor to social capital. While this issue clearly warrants further investigation, this analysis follows that used by Hall. He treats it as both, but concludes that social capital in Britain is not eroding because participation levels are being sustained, even though social trust has declined.

We would suggest that a number of different questions need to be raised when attempting to address this apparent paradox:

- Is the character of formal involvement changing such that it is less able to generate the social networks necessary for the creation of social capital?
- Is the distribution of membership and volunteering changing in ways that impede the development of social trust in society as a whole?

- What exactly is the nature of the relationship between participation and the development of social trust, and is the assumption -- that they are directly linked a valid one?
- Are there other key arenas for sociability and the generation of social networks that have been overlooked, and that might reflect different trends?
- Finally, are there other external factors which may have contributed to the decline in social trust whilst participation levels appear to be maintained?

Hall suggests that the answers may lie in a changing character of participation, distributional issues, and particular externalities, specifically perceptions of the economic climate and inequality, as well as growing individualism and moral relativism. We think it very likely that the character of participation - and thus its ability to generate social capital - has changed. We will argue that while the erosion of social trust may not be continuing, the current level is low compared to the past thirty or forty years. We believe this scenario may be the result of the following factors: widespread disparities in levels in formal participation that may strongly impede the creation of generalised social trust; there are other arenas which are increasingly important to the generation of social ties which are commonly overlooked, in particular the workplace and internet; and that there are also some significant externalities which may influence the situation, most especially sharply rising levels of inequality.

Trends in Social Capital

Hall adopts Putnam's narrowest definition of social capital as "networks of sociability, both formal and informal" (p420) in his review of social capital in Britain. In the formal sense Hall focuses on individual engagement with nonprofit or voluntary associations. In identifying informal networks of sociability, he looks at how people spend their time, and in particular their leisure time. Hall seems to distinguish the networks that make up social capital from the outcomes of social capital, which are "the trust the individuals feel towards others" (p418) and "their capacity to join together in collective action" (p418). He places a particular emphasis on participation in politics and active support for democracy. In these definitions and approach, he is drawing on Putnam but also trying to conceptualise social capital within a specifically British context.

Formal Engagement with Voluntary Associations

The level of social capital in a society or community is most often conceptualised as the level of formal engagement of individuals with voluntary or nonprofit organisations. Hall identifies three ways in which people engage formally with voluntary organisations:

as members of associations

as volunteers

as donors

In this section we look at more recent trends in these three forms of formal engagement, we well as identifying the limitations of some of the indicators that Hall uses. We then go onto discuss what these imply for Hall's conclusions about the resilience of social capital in Britain.

Membership in Voluntary Associations

Membership of voluntary organisations is suggested by Hall as a way of operationalising the face to face interaction in a common endeavour which is central to levels of social capital. Hall focuses on membership of voluntary associations, and calculates the average number of memberships per person in Britain to show a 44% increase in levels of membership between 1973 and 1990. We show that the membership data as presented by Hall does not accurately reflect the extent of membership of nonprofit organisations in Britain. There are two key problems with presenting the data in this way. Firstly it assumes that individuals with more memberships have more social capital and that this contributes to the overall level of social capital in the country. Secondly it gives an impression of rising overall membership levels, without representing the people who are not members at all.

Presenting the data as the proportion of people who are members, shows that levels of membership are stable rather than increasing. The data does support Hall's conclusions that the divide between the participation levels of the upper and lower socio-economic status groups is growing.

This increasing concentration of membership, raises questions about potential distributional issues, in particular depending on gender, age and socio-economic status. Not only is the average number of memberships the highest, but also the percentage of people who are members at all. Gender differences and differences in age are not as significant as social class.

Distribution issues are addressed by Johnston & Jowell (1999) in their review of social capital in Britain based on the British Social Attitudes Survey (BSAS). They find that the middle and upper middle classes are more than twice as likely to be members of at least one community organisation than unskilled manual workers. This is also reflected in the fact that people on higher incomes and owner occupiers are more often members. Even in sporting organisations and trade unions, which they comment are most likely to attract people from a wide range of social classes, membership is more common amongst the middle classes (p191).

The key point to consider at this stage is whether membership is becoming something that the people who are already members increasingly participate in, especially amongst the middle classes. We are presented with two increasingly divergent groups: the 'multi-members' who are largely drawn from AB, and C1 social classes, and the 'non-members' who come from C2, and DE. This raises issues about who is being left out, which tends to be people on lower incomes, with lower status jobs, or unemployed. In addition ethnic minority communities often experience higher levels of poverty and unemployment, as well as discrimination, and we would expect minority groups to participate in different associations and in different ways compared with the majority population.

In an analysis of levels of participation in Britain, the National Council for Voluntary Organisations/Centre for Civil Society commented that "for the unemployed, levels of participation are 14 percentage points lower than twenty years ago. Clearly, the voluntary sector has not been successful in actively involving this socially excluded part of society" (NCVO, 2000).

The lack of involvement of these people is an issue for them as they "probably have the most to gain from such activity" (Johnston & Jowell, 1999: p193). In addition we would argue that divisions within society are reflected in the uneven distribution of participation in voluntary associations, and that these divisions have an impact on all members of society in terms of levels of social capital, and in particular social trust.

A second point to consider is what the increasing concentration of membership could tell us about the changing nature of membership. In particular it may be that people are able to have more memberships because they are not active as members in terms of attending meetings and participating in a range of activities. A follow up of Hall's analysis of membership organisations from his 1999 paper, shows that membership is decreasing in organisations where you find face to face interaction in working towards a common endeavour (Cameron, 2001). At the same time membership in organisations where a private benefit is received, such as car or dangerous sports insurance, is increasing.

It may be that membership is increasingly being considered to be a product, for which certain benefits are received, rather than a commitment of support or involvement.

This 'commodification' has implications for the contribution that membership of voluntary associations can make to creating and maintaining social capital. If people are members without face to face interaction and networking potential, and motivated by personal benefits rather than social concerns, then we have to question how effectively membership contributes to social capital.

Volunteering

Volunteering is similarly considered important in assessing levels of social capital, and may be a more robust measure as it tends to require interaction with other people. Perhaps the most comprehensive recent survey on volunteering is the 1997 survey by the National Centre for Volunteering (NCV). It is therefore now possible to provide a more thorough review of the levels of volunteering than Hall was able to do.

Trends in the level and nature of volunteering have been most clearly identified by the National Centre for Volunteering in a series of surveys conducted in 1981, 1991 and 1997. The proportion of people participating in volunteering increased in the 1980s and has since levelled off. However the people who are volunteering, are giving more time than was given in the past, and the average time donation has risen from 2.7 hours per week in 1991 to 4 hours in 1997.

A concentration of volunteering activity is commented on by Johnston and Jowell (1999) in their review of social capital in Britain. They find that whilst 33% of their sample have volunteered at least once in the previous year, and 87% participate either as a volunteer or a member in at least one association, "the truly activist core" is less than 10% of the population (Johnston & Jowell, 1999: p185). Their conclusion is positive, "there clearly is still 'such a thing as society'" (p185), though they go on to express concern about the groups of people who are not participating in these forms of activity.

In terms of distributional issues, young people and ethnic minority groups tend to be less involved in formal volunteering. Little is known about how people from ethnic minorities engage as volunteers and their level of volunteering (ACU, 2000). The numbers of young people volunteering has decreased significantly since 1991. In addition young people are giving much less time than they used to when they do volunteer, 0.7 hours per week in 1997. Similarly younger people would prefer to give money than time, with 30% of 18 to 24 years olds agreeing compared with 25% of 25+ year olds (Matheson & Summerfield, 2000a).

The other significant distributional issue is that there has been a fall in volunteering amongst people who are unemployed, down from 50% in 1991 to 38% in 1997. This may indicate changes in the benefits system having made volunteering difficult for people dependent on benefits.

When considering volunteering then we see a similar pattern emerging as in membership levels. Fewer people are volunteering, but the ones that are, give more time. Young people and unemployed are increasingly not volunteering, but based on the survey quoted above we do not have clear reasons for this. In fact there is some evidence that young people have very positive attitudes to volunteering (Matheson & Summerfield, 2000a). This is supported by a 2002 survey of young people by the Charities Aid Foundation which found that 96% of young people intended to give money or time in the future (CAF, 2002), and many were already supporting charities through donations, sponsorship, gifts in kind, and recycling.

The reason why people are giving more time than in the past may be because active membership is now being labelled volunteering.

In addition it may reflect the professionalisation of the management of volunteering, where volunteers have to make more definite time commitments as charities invest more in their training. Again this raises questions about the changing nature of volunteering and what this might mean for the nature and level of social capital for different groups. As volunteering becomes increasingly professionalised, this has implications for who participates, why and how.

Charitable Giving

Charitable giving is mentioned by Hall almost in passing as an element of charitable endeavour (p425). Britain has a long charitable tradition dating from the sixteenth century, and there is widespread participation from people of all classes in charitable giving. Hall talks about giving as having "risen steadily" (p425) to £5 billion in total, or £10 per person in 1993.

These figures provided him with further confidence regarding participation and the state of social capital. However the picture changed significantly after 1993. In fact, despite an improved economy, levels of giving fell between 1993 and 1999/2000. Major government policies encouraging giving were introduced in 2000, and levels have begun to climb. Over the past twenty years, whilst the average donation has increased, participation in giving has fallen to 67.5% (2000) of the population, from 81% (1981). (NCVO, 2000)

Amounts given are closely related to social class, with AB giving the most, and then C1, C2, DE and unemployed people. People of higher socio-economic status are more likely to have money to give, and are more likely to be targets for fundraising. However it is also true that people on lower incomes give more proportionately than would be expected based on income level alone. Indeed, average giving levels as a percentage of income are greatest for those with least income. This reflects in part the dominance of 'spare change' giving methods such as street collections, which encourage broad participation, but low average gifts, even among the well off (Wright, 2001). Such methods have come under increasing competition from the National Lottery in Britain, which presents itself as a an opportunity to support charitable causes.

Giving levels are employed as evidence of the relative strength of social capital (Putnam, 2000) although there is dispute about whether charitable giving can help create social capital. Hall reflects this somewhat ambiguous treatment of giving, nevertheless using it as an indicator of the presence of social capital.

This results from the strong emphasis among many authors, including Hall, on the necessity of face to face interaction for the creation of social capital. However, we would suggest that financial contributions could well serve as the basis for some form of reciprocal activity which contributes to the formation of relationships and networks, the support of common endeavour, and therefore to social capital.

OVERALL TRENDS IN FORMAL ENGAGEMENT WITH VOLUNTARY ORGANISATIONS

There are two broad trends that are easily identified from the specific activities outlined above. Firstly there is a tendency for membership, volunteering and giving to become more concentrated within the middle classes, reflecting a distribution issue. There is relatively little known about the ways in which different minority communities in Britain engage in such formal networking , for example elderly people, ethnic minorities etc, but we would expect that many such groups experience barriers to some of the key forms of participation. Secondly there has been a tendency within the voluntary sector as a whole to become more professionalised.

This has led in part to consumer based approaches that increasingly focus on individual private benefits and specific benefits for the voluntary organisations in order to encourage participation, rather than on social or community benefits. This may mean that the nature of the engagement is changing, and for example membership becomes more like purchasing a product than a means of social engagement, and volunteering becomes a way of advancing a career.

This is also taking place within a context of government interest in the sector. Under New Labour, Britain has seen a number of government led policies which are intended to encourage citizen engagement, for example through increasing volunteering and giving. This goes alongside interest in increasing the capacity of the sector to provide government contracted services. The delicate balance between government interest, support and interference of the voluntary sector influences the ways in which people experience their engagement with associations as self generated and directed, or as managed and part of government.

Informal Sociability

Formal involvement in voluntary associations is "only a small part of a complex web of social ties and activities that make for a healthy society" (Johnston & Jowell, 1999: p190). Hall also suggests that informal sociability can be a very significant way in which people are engaged in and form social networks, though measuring it is difficult. We have identified three main issues that directly effect social capital: the amount of time people have available for socialising; the content of that socialising; and the distribution across gender, age and socio-economic status.

The amount of available leisure time is a critical factor in the capacity of people to participate socially and politically. Hall (p272) identified an increase in leisure time between 1961 and 1984 due to reduced working hours and the use of labour saving devices in the home. In particular he noted that the extra leisure time is spent outside of the home, and extending the figures to 1995 shows the same trend. However the increase is small, such that in 1995 people had only an average of 20 minutes per day more leisure than they had in 1961 (Gershuny & Fisher, 2000).

The content of what people do in their leisure time and where they spend it is also significant. There is a clear trend for people to spend less time at home, and in particular less time eating meals at home and more time going out and socialising, as indicated.

Though questioned by Hall, the main activity generally thought to mitigate against socialising is watching TV. In fact TV watching and radio listening have remained roughly level in the past forty years (Gershuny & Fisher, 2000). It should also be noted that the effect of TV is not entirely anti-social, as popular culture in the form of TV programmes can provide a common basis for immediate and subsequent interaction.

In terms of "pursuits associated with social capital" (Hall: 426), Hall identifies sport, civic duties, social clubs, pubs, and visits to friends. These activities seem likely to indicate some level of socialising. In particular Hall comments that the proportion of the population visiting pubs has increased, especially amongst women who were often excluded from these forms of socialising. Visiting other people, or being visited, is something that between 95% and 100% of people do each month, and is stable at about 35 to 40 minutes per day (Matheson & Summerfield, 2001; Gershuny & Fisher, 2000: p646). Longer trips to visit friends and relatives increased by 88% between 1989 and 1999, from about 22% of the population to 44% (Matheson & Babb, 2002). Certainly current trends indicate that socialising with friends is healthy and thriving.

However this leaves a question about exactly who is socialising so actively in these ways. A significant weakness of the figures quoted by Hall, which include a range of social activities, is that they do not cover people who are not working: for example retired people, students, housewives, unemployed, and people who cannot work through illness or disability. These distributional issues reflect what we found in the more formal participation in voluntary associations - that certain groups of people are not fully participating in the range of the activities identified as important to social capital.

This supports Hall's concern that social capital is concentrated amongst the middle and upper middle classes, and that the working classes are experiencing an erosion of social solidarity and cohesion reflected in decreasing levels of social capital. At the same time, the measurements used may specify forms of participation which are most relevant to the middle and upper middle classes of society. This in turn may mean that our conceptualisation of social capital is simply not yet adequate to identifying forms of social capital in different groups of society. Intuition tells us that this is likely to be especially true for ethnic minority communities in Britain, where we would expect to see different types of relationships, networks and interactions between people.

Similarly social capital amongst women is inadequately understood and researched. Women as a whole spend more time on household duties such as childcare, shopping, cooking and cleaning and in 1995 had fully 50 minutes less leisure time than men - though this gap is closing (Gershuny & Fisher, 2000). Moreover, as Vivien Lowndes (1999, 2002) argues forcefully, women engage in highly reciprocal networks, for example sharing child care, which are generally ignored in standard categories and assessments of engagement. Furthermore, such engagement challenges the standard equation of informal engagement with leisure pursuits, reinforcing the suspicion raised above that the forms of even informal sociability being literally 'counted' will miss the often quite distinct patterns of ethnic and religious minorities.

The recent trends outlined above are consistent with Hall's findings, that levels of socialising are in general stable and seem even to be increasing slowly but steadily. There are two main issues that warrant further consideration and analysis. Firstly that the distribution of informal sociability as seeming to be concentrated within the middle classes; and secondly that there may be important forms of socialising amongst the working classes, women, and ethnic minorities that are not being picked up with current measurements.

Social Trust

Social trust is considered by many authors to be a key element of social capital, and is also considered by some to be a benefit or outcome of social capital (Johnston & Jowell,

1999). Peter Hall relies on the World Values Survey from 1980-1995 along with previous surveys to document levels of generalised social trust. Hall concludes that "the one indicator for social capital that has fallen over the post-war years is that heavily qualify) Hall reports significant declines in trust between 1990 and 1995.

The decline of social trust in the EVS data from 44% of the population in 1990 to 30% in 1995 represents a real decline of just over 14% in just five years, nearly identical to the drop in trust in the United States during the same period. In fact, the relative decline in trust in the UK was 33%, slightly above the US decline of 30%. The large - and similarly patterned - drops in these two countries contrast with the overall trend in nine western countries in which trust fell slightly during the same period, and in the case of West Germany and Norway, increased slightly.

However, more recent EVS data for Britain indicates that at least as of 1999, the decline in trust has not continued, but instead plateaued when compared with 1995 figures. Future figures will be required to know what this development might mean, and whether the 1999 figures reflect slowing decline, stabilisation, or perhaps a change in direction.

The British Social Attitudes Survey, has reported relatively stable levels of trust at around 43% of the population since 1997. Both surveys base their trust levels on answers to a single question: "Generally speaking, would you say that most people can be trusted or that you can't be too careful in dealing with people?" (exact wording taken from European Values Survey). While consistently somewhat higher than the EVS figures, the figures from the British Social Attitudes Survey which was begun in 1997, are not necessarily inconsistent with them. Both surveys appear to reflect an arresting of the decline in social trust between

1997 and 2000, and the differences between them may simply reflect a survey 'house effect.'

At the same time the distribution of trust is important. As might be expected social trust measured by the EVS in 1981, 1990 and1999 is consistently higher than average within the socio-economic status groups of A, B, and C1. Within the C2, D, and E groups it is consistently lower than the average.

We would argue that this sole question may be unable to provide an entirely adequate base for an assessment of generalised trust across a society without other data. We would suggest the possible use of an index of questions, including measures such as reciprocity, to provide more solid footings for analysis.

CAUSAL EXPLANATIONS FOR CHANGES IN LEVELS OF SOCIAL CAPITAL

The paradox that Hall has sought to explain is the maintenance of participation coupled with the decline in social trust. He draws on a wide range of arguments on the changing nature of society and the impact of the state to identify reasons why this apparent paradox has arisen in the UK. His argument is comprehensive, examining class mobility, industrialisation, the women's movement, the educational revolution. In particular Hall emphasises the role of the state in improving education, enabling and encouraging social mobility and providing the framework for economic prosperity.

Over twenty years of rhetoric and policy emphasising individual initiative and class mobility has seen a rise in the predominance of the middle classes, both in terms of values and a growing proportion of the population. Nevertheless our examination of participation patterns in Britain leads us to conclude that class based divisions at this point in time still show remarkable strength and resiliency. In fact 68% of the population view themselves as 'working class and proud of it', including 55% of people who would otherwise be categorised as middle class (MORI, 2002). The social institutions that were the mainstay of working class participation - mutual aid societies, clubs, labour unions - have disappeared or changed, and the demise of such institutions means that exposure to the habits and values of participation will be far less likely.

We agree with Hall that government policy is critically important. There are a number of arenas where it can either support or constrain the formation of social connections. Education (as mentioned by Hall) is important. But despite dramatically widening access to higher education so that now some 33% of the population has had a university education, we think that on the whole the fragmented British educational system tends to reinforce rather than rectify class divisions. And there are other critical areas that are often overlooked. Transport - its speed, reliability, and cost - is a significant factor, and without good quality options a wide range of connections are impeded. The availability of affordable child care and family friendly policies are necessary for the participation of carers, mostly women. Labour standards, particularly working hours and conditions, can also encourage or constrain participation.

In addition to these necessary conditions are policies which bear directly on social participation. These have been a particular priority of the Labour government elected in 1997. It has had a vision of (re)creating 'civic community,' establishing an Active Communities Unit, and instituting policies to encourage volunteering, charitable giving, and local civic engagement. It has also 'embraced' the voluntary sector. A partnership between the sectors led to the introduction of the 'Compact' which sets out the principles governing the relationship between government and voluntary organisations. In the autumn of 2002, the Treasury and the Cabinet Office produced reports, both outlining new policies on the roles, financing and legal structures of voluntary organisations emphasising their significance to government thinking.

One of Hall's arguments is that the decline in social trust can be explained by the trend towards individualism in society. The emphasis on the promise of individual achievement was a hallmark of government rhetoric and policy during the 18 years of Conservative governments led by Margaret Thatcher and John Major. Hall suggests that the rise in individualism is illustrated by increasing levels of moral relativism, operationalised in the European values survey by a question asking whether there are 'clear guidelines on what is good and evil whatever the circumstances', or whether this depends on the context. We are not convinced by the proposed relationship between individualism and moral relativism, nor the assumption that moral relativism equals or implies a lack of consideration for others.

Moreover the data from the European Values Survey indicate the opposite of Hall's finding - while relativists outnumber absolutists, there has been in fact a clear decline in moral relativism and a rise in moral absolutism over the past twenty years. However we would not therefore suggest that somehow Britain is becoming less individualistic, merely that 'relativism' can't be used as a proxy for 'individualism.'.

However there does seem to be potential in greater analysis of the role of specific values, for example individual self-reliance and social duty, etc., in contributing to or impeding the development of social capital. Hall looks at a number of 'moral' dilemmas such as whether people think it is ever justified to accept a bribe or cheat on their taxes. Whilst Hall shows an increase in self-regarding attitudes, we have found that the increase over the past 20 years is marginal. The one area where there is a noticably change is that more people think avoiding paying a fare on public transport can be justified - which may reflect more on the level of service than on changing values. However we do believe that values are important, but that the trends and relationships between them are more complex than Hall suggested

Hall provides an insightful analysis of the social forces he thinks may explain the paradox regarding trust and participation. He focuses on the role of changing values and the impact of government policy on social change and individual attitudes. He also details the effect of a sense of economical prosperity on levels of interpersonal social trust, such that in economic downturns social trust declines. However he does not place an emphasis on the role of the market and the workplace in contributing to the changing nature of society and the frameworks within which people and communities live. The workplace is not only significant as a place where people form meaningful connections, but also has a broader impact on social values and changes in society, and the promulgation of employment policies and practices.

In this vein, one of the trends that we consider important is change in the nature of work and the impact this has had on levels of financial and personal security and satisfaction. The late 80s and early 90s not only saw high levels of unemployment, and with it a challenge to people's understanding of job security, but also increases in self-employment, part-time work and temporary contracts (Galley, D., 2000). Along with this came reports of higher levels of stress (Galley, D., 2000). However between 1996 and 2001 levels of work related stress and concern over the work-life balance reduced amongst almost all working people (Gallie & Paugan, 2002). People on fixed term contracts were more likely to feel insecure in their work, but also reported greater job satisfaction (Matheson & Babb, 2002).

Similarly, during the period when social trust seems to have levelled out, dissatisfaction with life and psychological distress went down, and this is thought to be mainly associated with people shifting from unemployment into work (Gallie & Paugan, 2002). There are two main interwoven trends that have taken place: the economic upturn and reduction in numbers unemployed, and the changing perceptions of work as increasingly offering less security at the same time as providing more opportunities. There is a delicate balance between the opening up of opportunities and freedoms at work for individuals, and the economic climate and what Hall terms the 'national confidence effects arising from broader perceptions of the economy'. We would therefore argue that the changing nature of the work environment should be investigated more seriously when attempting to identify the causes of the changing levels of generalised social trust.

INEQUALITY

Inequality in Britain has increased considerably in the past twenty years. The increase in income inequality between the mid 1980s and early 1990s was over 20%, the largest percentage increase in any country surveyed, including the United States (Mule, 1998) In 1995 the UK had the highest level of inequality in the EU, but slightly lower than the US (British Social Attitudes Survey, 1986). Inequality increased most significantly during the 1980s; this is attributed concurrently to rising earnings and increased household unemployment, followed by a reduction in redistribution through the taxation system (Atkinson, 2000: p376). In the first half of the 1990s income inequality stabilised, but in the latter part of the 1990s, inequality increased again (Matheson & Summerfield, 2001).

While the growth in inequality is dramatic, it is actually the perception of large and growing inequality that should provide the most direct link to the sharply falling levels of generalised social trust between 1990 and 1995. And in fact that is exactly what occurred. The British Social Attitudes Survey reports public perceptions that levels of poverty were increasing, and that there was a growing gap between rich and poor - particularly between 1990 and 1995 (We can reference the chapter by Hill? in last year's BSAS report)- Furthermore, evidence suggests that people in Britain generally value equity and are bothered by increases in income inequality more than in some other countries, especially the United States. (Alesina, Di Tella, & MacCulloch, 2001)

We propose that these increases in inequality are likely to affect the levels of social trust, and what used to be referred to as the sense of social cohesion. Uslaner suggests that it is harder to trust 'outsider' groups when there is greater inequality. In other words it is always easier to trust the people you know and can relate to as your 'own kind', but when there is increased inequality it becomes harder to trust those who are not your 'own kind'. You are also less likely to generalise your trust of people you know to those you do not know. We suggest that is it this form of trust that has decreased as income inequality has increased.

It is not only the people on the lower incomes who are adversely affected in some way, sometimes even the people who have gained financially may have experienced some disadvantages in other areas: "For many, increased income has come at the price of insecurity" (Barclay, 1995: p9). In addition Barclay goes on to argue that "Regardless of any moral arguments or feelings of altruism everyone shares an interest in the cohesiveness of society. As the gaps between rich and poor grow, the problems of the marginalized groups which are being left behind rebound on the more comfortable majority." (Barclay, 1995: p8). As well as affecting social trust, income inequality could also impact on social capital in terms of the nature of the relationships and networks between people.

It may be that the rise in income inequality has exacerbated class differences that had become less significant since the Second World War. Hall argues that the growing individualism in society and the shift away from more collectivist forms means that "social relations became less oriented around class divisions and more oriented to individual achievement" (Hall, 1999: p446). In fact our findings indicate the strongly resilient effect of social class and the increasing exclusion of many people from the forms of social capital that are most commonly conceptualised - engagement in voluntary associations and political engagement.

At the same time, it may also be the case that increasing individualism and a decreasing collective sense of mutual obligation are themselves contributing to growing inequality. Robert Putnam has suggested that when social capital is high, values of reciprocity and community will be strong, making both extremely high and extremely low levels of income socially unacceptable.

In such a context, people will be embarrassed by having and displaying substantially greater resources than those around them, and at the same time be highly uncomfortable about others having very little. Anthony Atkinson also argues for the often neglected importance of social norms in reducing inequality (Atkinson, 2001). We think it plausible that high levels of social capital would likely constrain the extremes of income inequality, and further that the relationship between equality and social capital may be a reciprocal one (Aldridge & Halpern, 2002).

DISCUSSION AND CONCLUSION

In contrast to Robert Putnam's claim that social capital in America is in decline, Peter Hall's assessment of the state of social capital in Britain is that it is on the a whole robust one, with consistently high levels of social and political participation. He finds the dropping levels of social trust worrisome, as is the uneven distribution of participation, but finds reassurance in what seemed to be increasing levels of giving, and comparatively high levels of political participation.

Our analysis suggests a somewhat darker picture. With the withering of many active working class institutions over the past twenty years, formal participation is increasingly concentrated among certain (class based) groups - those who are active in everything. Its character is becoming increasingly commodified, chosen as a private good and negotiated at a distance without personal interaction. On the other hand, there are indications of new arenas in which ties and networks form - as well as traditional arenas that have been largely ignored. While expansion of education and active government support of participation - particularly in the past four years - may well have had an effect of encouraging participation, we would argue that the class based divisions which constrain participation remain deeply imbedded and result in significant drag to efforts to increase and broaden social capital. The distribution of participation is not a niggling concern - it is the main story, with important implications for social trust as well. The changing nature of working life and sharply growing inequality are coincident with the sharpest drop in trust in the post war period, very possibly undermining efforts to create links across society and a feeling of social cohesion. We are less convinced than Peter Hall that the state of social capital in Britain is indeed robust, and believe that 'old fashioned' concerns about inequality, social class, and workplace protections, may actually be critical to effective strategies to support the development of social capital.

We would conclude, contrary to Hall's analysis, that Britain indeed may have experienced a decline in 'social capital' strikingly similar to that of the United States. Hall argues that despite declining levels of generalised social trust, participation in associational life remains robust in Britain. We believe that if you look below the simple averages, there are two fundamental factors which undermine the effectiveness of modern civic participation to generate trust across society. The first is the increasing concentration of participation - largely in the A,B, and C1 social classes. The second is the commodification of membership and volunteering, making it increasingly about private benefit, hollowing out its social meaning, and weakening its relationship with social capital. This was the end of a long period of political and policy commitment to individualism under the Thatcher and Major governments. It was also during this period that income inequality had grown significantly, and that the perception of inequality peaked in Britian.

A social divide that is strikingly absent from both Hall's and our own analysis is that between minority ethnic groups and the majority population in Britain. This is evident, not by an analysis of associational membership, but by the riots and violence in a number of different communities throughout the country during 2001 and by the concerns about institutional racism. This has coincided with public anxiety around immigration and at times media villification of asylum seekers in Britain, but also in 'Fortress' Europe more widely. It would not be surprising to conclude that the public mood and media rhetoric would reduce levels of social trust within a racially diverse country such as Britain, though would not necessarily reduce levels of bonding social capital between people from similar backgrounds.

Both Britain and America again show similar apparent plateauing in levels of social trust in 1999. It is too early to tell whether this is an anomaly in an overall downward trend, or a point in a further increasing pattern. We would speculate that the 1999/2000 figures could in Britain reflect the general optimism of the period after the election of the Labour government, and the rhetorical shift from individualism to Third Way doctrines which explicitly embraced social concerns.

One of the elements that Hall highlights in his definition of social capital is the importance of relative equality among participants. Unlike America's mythology of a classless society, Britain's forms and arenas for participation have evolved in quite distinct - and class-based - directions. Upper classes were imbued with 'noblesse oblige' responsibilities. The middle classes dominated the practices and organisations dedicated to philanthropy, seen in Britain as selfless giving to those less fortunate. Both the practice of philanthropy and the term itself have been seen in the twentieth century as patronising, archaic, and exemplifying unequal social relations. (Beveridge, 1946, Wright, 2001) The working class tradition of mutual aid organisations and trade unions was by contrast far more reciprocal and egalitarian, but these insitutions were severely weakened and in some cases eliminated by the de-industrialisation and union busting of the past twenty years.

Finally, while Britain does have a long history of voluntary association and what Hall refers to as charitable endeavor, it is not enirely clear that these are the most salient arenas for the creation of networked relationships and bonds of mutuality and trust at this point in time. While it is tempting to apply the kinds of analysis to Britain that have been used in the US where the associational model is uniquely pervasive, it may not be the best or most accurate way to approach an assessment of the state of social capital in other social and cultural contexts. Compared to many places, Britain and America are relatively similar. Other contexts can be expected to differ to a much greater extent.

COOPERATION WITH REGIONAL NGOS IN SOUTH ASIA

SAARC has emphasised the need for strengthening inter-governmental efforts with increased people-to- people contacts through greater participation of NGOs, including professional bodies in the private sector, to promote socio-economic and cultural development of South Asia. In appreciation of the contributions of the NGOs and professional bodies to the official SAARC process, SAARC has set in motion a process of granting recognition to such deserving bodies. These organisations fall under two categories: (a) SAARC Regional Apex Bodies, and (b) SAARC Recognised Bodies.

SAARC REGIONAL APEX BODIES

1. SAARC Chamber of Commerce and Industry (SCCI)

The SAARC Chamber of Commerce and Industry (SCCI) was granted the status of SAARC Regional Apex Body in December 1992. The SCCI brings together the national chambers of commerce and industry of the seven SAARC countries under one umbrella.

The SCCI has played a significant role in promoting the core area of economic and trade cooperation in the region. It was instrumental in bringing into fruition the SAARC Preferential Trading Arrangement (SAPTA).

SCCI has been very active in the promotion of trade and interaction of business community of the SAARC region. It organises the SAARC Economic Cooperation Conferences on a regular basis and so far has held two such conferences in New Delhi (November, 1996), and Islamabad (March, 1998). SCCI has also been organising SAARC Trade Fairs in Member Countries, the first of which was held in New Delhi in January 1996. The Second Fair was held in Colombo in 1998 and the next SAARC Trade Fair is expected to be held in Islamabad in 1999.

SCCI has established a permanent Secretariat, headed by a Secretary-General, located in Pakistan.

Saarc Law

SAARCLAW is an Association for persons of the legal communities of SAARC countries. It was established in 1991 and was accorded recognition as a SAARC Regional Apex Body in July 1994. It was established with the twin objectives of bringing together the legal Communities of the region for closer cooperation and developing law as a source of social change for development. SAARCLAW has been convening periodic conferences covering important areas of common interest to Member States.

These conferences focused on themes such as : law and development in the region; law as an instrument of social justice; law as an instrument of economic change; law and justice for the common people; and development through law; legal education; public interest litigation; money laundering; child abuse and violence against women and investment climate in the region.

Since 1995, a parallel meeting of the Chief Justices of the Member States has also been held to coincide with the SAARCLAW conference. SAARCLAW aims at, inter-alia, exchange of legal professionals, establishment of SAARCLAW libraries, and harmonisation of laws which offer mutual assistance within the judicial process. The Secretariat of the SAARCLAW is located in Sri Lanka.

SAARC RECOGNISED BODIES

1. South Asian Association for Regional Cooperation of Architects (SAARCH)

The SAARCH was founded in 1991 in Colombo with the objective of assisting the development of national architectural bodies within the South Asian region so that it would provide opportunities for consultation on holding of conferences of architects to discuss professional matters and interchange ideas. SAARCH was granted SAARC Recognised Body status in May 1997. It has held several conferences in the region and also publishes a newsletter SAARCH . The SAARCH Secretariat is located in Sri Lanka.

2. Association of Management Development Institutions (AMDISA)

AMDISA was established in June 1988 for the promotion of management education and management development activities in South Asian region. It has brought under its umbrella the leading institutions, both public and private, involved in the teaching, training and research in management and development oriented fields. SAARC Recognised Body status was granted to AMDISA in May 1997 in recognition of its contribution to management and development education fields. AMDISA has held several fora on management development related topics. Its general office is located in India.

3. SAARC Federation of University Women (SAARCFUW)

SAARCFUW was established in July 1995 in Colombo with the objectives of, among other things, bringing together the university women of the region to promote understanding and cooperation and share responsibility in society for the social upliftment in the region. SAARCFUW was granted the status of SAARC recognised body in May 1997.

At present, it has national chapters in Bangladesh, India, Nepal, Pakistan and Sri Lanka. It publishes a newsletter SAARCFUW. SAARCFUW Secretariat is currently located in Sri Lanka.

4.South Asian Federation of Accountants (SAFA)

SAFA was established in 1984 with the objective of developing a coordinated accountancy profession in the region. Its membership is open to accountancy bodies in the South Asian region. At present the Institutes of Chartered Accountants and/or the Institutes of Cost and Management Accountants in Bangladesh, India, Pakistan and Sri Lanka are the members of SAFA. SAFA was granted the status of SAARC Recognised Body in May 1997.

Its Secretariat is located at South Asian Federation and Accountants, Institute of Chartered Accountants of India.

5. SAARC Association of Town Planners

SAARC Association of Town Planners was granted SAARC recognition in August 1998. The main objective of the Association is to promote coordinated town planning in the region.

At present, its country chapters are in Bangladesh, India, Pakistan and Sri Lanka. Its headquarters is located in Colombo.

6. SAARC Cardiac Society

SAARC Cardiac Society was granted the status of SAARC recognised body in November 1998. The main objectives of the Society is to foster cooperation and exchange of information in the field of cardiovascular science including its research, training and rehabilitation programmes. It has country chapters in Bangladesh, India, Nepal, Pakistan and Sri Lanka. Its headquarters is located at Dhaka.

7. Association of SAARC Speakers and Parliamentarians

The Association of SAARC Speakers and Parliamentarians was formally launched in 1992 in Kathmandu. The Heads of State or Government at their Seventh SAARC Summit (Dhaka, April 1993) welcomed the initiative of the Speakers of Parliaments of SAARC countries in forming the Association.

6

NGOs in Nepal

Regional Meeting on Prevention of Trafficking of Girls and Women — Center for Legal Research and Resource Development

Background of the Project

In the past decade, over 200,000 Nepali girls and women have been trafficked to India and beyond for sexual exploitation. The clandestine nature of trafficking makes it difficult to obtain accurate figures, however trafficking of women and especially of children is on the rise.

Poverty and the lack of income-earning opportunities outside marriage for women and girls have led to an increase in the pool of recruits for trafficking. Many women and girls are lured by promises of jobs and fake marriages and can be recruited by family members, co-workers, and friends.

For widowed, divorced, or abandoned women prostitution may be the only way tc access economic resources. Violence against girls and women by husbands and other members of the household as well as by members of the community has also been identified as a major cause for pushing women into prostitution, especially in low-caste households.

As female virginity is highly valued in Nepal, trafficking of women and (mostly female) children renders them undesirable candidates for marriage. Women may be forced by economic necessity into prostitution later in life as the result of having earlier been raped or sold.

The low status of women in Nepal produces the conditions under which trafficking, gender-based violence, and prostitution "by choice" occur.

Structural gender inequality is evidenced by women's and girls' high rates of illiteracy, their poor health, and their limited access to resources. Women's low status is also a factor behind ineffective government policies and corrupt or indifferent police who do little to prevent trafficking. Moreover, the women and children are often penalized instead of the traffickers or their clients.

Relevant government and nongovernment organizations (NGOs) have been slow to adopt a coordinated, regional approach to curb cross-border trafficking.

Trafficking is a regional issue involving more than one national jurisdiction. For this reason and with funding from the Asian Development Bank, the Center for Legal Research and Resource Development (CeLRRd) brought together a number of government and nongovernment organizations from Bangladesh, India, and Nepal in order to discuss strategies to eradicate trafficking at the regional level. The Regional Consultation Meeting on Prevention of Trafficking of Girls and Women was held on 22-24 February, 2001 in Kathmandu.

Project Objectives and Scope

The primary objectives of the meeting were the following:

- to initiate and facilitate networking and coordination of governments and NGOs for a regional response to trafficking

- to expedite the adoption of the South Asian Association for Regional Cooperation (SAARC) regional convention against trafficking
- to generate support for NGOs in Nepal to intercept girls and women from traffickers
- to create a resolution to draw the attention of the Governments of India and Nepal to address urgently the issue of trafficking
- to mobilize the officials of SAARC countries to address the problem of trafficking at the regional level
- to identify mechanisms for rescuing victims

The 3-day conference was attended by participants from Bangladesh, India, Nepal, Sweden, and Thailand. They represented governments, national and international NGOs, and multilateral organizations active in anti-trafficking initiatives. A special feature of the meeting was the inclusion of local participants, representatives from paralegal committees active in trafficking-affected districts, and school teachers and local elected representatives. The paralegal women contributed experiences and concerns gained while building the Community Surveillance System Against Trafficking (CSSAT), a project designed and implemented by CeLRRd over the previous 7 years.

On the first day of the conference, proceedings were directed to briefings from each participant about their programs, their area of coverage, and strategies they had adopted to combat trafficking. Many common problems and strategies were identified. The lack of cooperation within and across borders was described as one of the factors hindering national and regional prevention. The tendency of organizations to work in isolation worked against the need for an efficient network. Isolation was also identified as a problem in the concentration on treating rescued victims without addressing community awareness, attitudes, and education. Recommendations included the need for

- cooperation among organizations working in places of origin and destination
- cooperation among organizations and border police
- greater awareness among parents about the protection and rights of their children
- increased awareness of trafficking among school children, teachers, and other members of society
- counseling parents to be more receptive toward reintegrating daughters into the society

The need for sensitizing police, the judiciary, and the media was stressed in order to protect and advance the rights of girls and women.

On the second and third days of the conference, country presentations were made. The need for a clear working definition of trafficking was raised as presenters noted that many definitions were vague, ambiguous, and "offender friendly." The need to take seriously the human rights violations of victims was also stressed. This would include the removal of laws that directly or indirectly discriminate against women and children, adequate representation of victims in court, and protection of victims of trafficking from exposure to public humiliation. Again, the presentations revealed many similarities in the concerns and strategies of the participating countries.

In the final session, the participants got together to chart recommendations for further action. Three groups focused on

- strengthening information networks among countries, government organizations, national and international NGOs, donors, and individual activists

- strengthening coordination for the protection of vulnerable girls and women
- launching advocacy for the prevention of trafficking at the regional level

Project Outcomes

The meeting was considered a huge success by all participants and achieved its primary goal by bringing together different organizations and countries to establish cross-border communication about trafficking and to share ideas, insights, and approaches. The representatives were especially appreciative of the inclusion of local participants working at the grassroots level noting that their perspective was often excluded from such forums. Meeting the paralegal representatives afforded all the opportunity to learn about their work and so impressed a representative from Bangladesh that the CSSAT program will be implemented in that country also. Participants also expressed great appreciation for the opportunity to network with other organizations and with individuals working in the field and considered the meeting a new beginning to addressing trafficking in South Asia.

Participants agreed to a number of recommendations in relation to strengthening networks, regional coordination, and regional approaches to prevent trafficking.

Recommendations to Strengthen the Network Included

- collection of data on missing persons with measures to report to local authorities or police
- identification of the trafficker to be followed by court trial and prosecution
- identification of communities and areas that are susceptible to trafficking

- identification of trafficking routes
- identification of times and seasons when trafficking is more likely to occur
- identification of the methods of trafficking

Recommendations to Strengthen Coordination Included

- networking among the state (district), national, and regional levels by taking down addresses, fax numbers, e-mail addresses, phone numbers, and contact points
- establishing communications at the grassroots, nationals, and regional levels
- arranging for feedback sessions at the grassroots, national, and regional levels
- translation of information at the national level
- sensitization of the judiciary and police
- establishment of resource centers

Recommendations to Prevent Trafficking at the Regional Level Included

- formation of national and international trafficking taskforces
- the inclusion in NGO national taskforces of human rights organizations
- the inclusion on the regional taskforce of representatives from SAARC nations
- the review and monitoring of each country's national plan of action against trafficking

These recommendations are to be achieved through a variety of measures including networking among SAARC members, collection and compilation of data, establishment of a regional court to handle trafficking issues through the SAARC secretariat/offices in each country, and special police to deal with trafficking. The participants also recommended actions to combat negative cultural values that promote trafficking by reinforcing the low status of women or that blame the victims. It was suggested that this could be achieved largely through cultural means such as movies, street plays, songs, radio, speeches, and meetings.

CIVIL SOCIETY IN NEPALESE CONTEXT: MEDIA PERSPECTIVE

The emergence of civil societies as a sub-culture within vibrant democratic societies are but one of the vivid manifestations of changing social values and adjustments spurred up by the impact of modern information systems. In other words, the dynamism of a civil social structure is unthinkable in the absence of free, information saturated and pluralistic information system. Implicitly, in transitional democracies, societies are evolving constantly until the ideal conditions of a civil society are achieved.

Among the fold of transitional democracies, too, there are dichotomies in levels and inculcation of values, which are determined by the level of economic development. For example, the problems faced by transitional democracies of former Soviet bloc countries are definitely different from the situation of less developed countries with poorly developed infrastructure. Indiscipline, corruption and bribery and political leaders with debased morality are some serious challenges facing the institutional development of democracy.

As the reputation of formal political institutions are tarnished with corruption, institutions within the framework of civil society are either too weak to create a viable alternative or not fully equipped with such situations.

Furthermore, many of the non-governmental organizations themselves might not have succeeded in establishing or emulating examples of good conduct as a model of excellence to be followed by others in the society.

The situation could be inversely improved a great deal with the presence of a very vigilant and active media system. But this requires, first, an information saturated society with assured access of the people to multiple channels of communication, thus, the universalization of access to channels of information, above all, should assume paramount importance in the consolidation of institutions under a civil society whose ultimate goal should be the overall improvement in the quality of human life.

Civil Society in Nepalese Context

Nepal has undergone a four-decade long period of bickering and experimentation with various forms of governments. The popular revolution of 1950 ushered in an era of a multi-party system of democracy, which lasted for a decade. It was followed by a 30-year long mono-party rule of Panchayat system, which outlawed the functioning of political parties. During this period non-governmental organizations and voluntary social movements did take root but had to be the object of strict surveillance of the authorities in power. Registration of organizations was based on arbitrary consideration rather than on uniform rules. While officially sanctioned organizations—the Panchayats and their affiliates flourished, other voluntary suffered a stunted growth.

The situation was not conducive for the growth of a free presses either. The Panchayat constitution required the media to be non-partisan and on this ground, registrations were concealed very often in the case of those raising the voice of dissent. In the face of these severe restrictions, the number of newspapers during the period of the first two decades (1960-1980) fluctuated between 27 to 84, while state-sector media organizations flourished. During the period of 1980 to 1990, control on the registration of newspapers was relaxed resulting in a five-fold increase of newspapers, but the restrictions still persisted. The private sector media had to struggle for survival by comprising their stakes with the authorities in power.

Against the background of trials and tribulations, the restoration of multi-party democracy in April 1990 was a major landmark in opening up a new era of liberalism, freedom and development in the country. The constitutional provisions on human rights, more specifically on press freedom, are more liberal; and elaborate when compared to Third World countries. In addition to Article 12.2, which provides for freedom of expression and opinion, Article 13 is more exclusive and elaborate on the Press and Publication Right of citizens. The Article provides guarantees against censorship of news items, articles or other reading material; against seizure or closure of a press for printing any news item, article or material; against cancellation or registration of a newspaper or periodical. Similarly, Article 16 has guaranteed the right to information of the people on matters of public importance.

In the aftermath of freedom, while voluntary non-governmental organizations of various hues and dimensions have grown in stature, political parties have not fared well in leading the country to the path of economic progress. The number of social organizations is stated to be around 6000 and spread all over the country. These are in addition to the already existing hierarchical order of various political parties, their frontal vocational or class organizations, trade unions, student organizations and the network of quasi-governmental local and municipal organizations. The increased influence and reach of NGOs, some sarcastically opine, is akin to running a parallel governmental outside the control and surveillance of official agencies. Some of the NGOs are emerging into powerful pressure groups and advocating for sweeping changes in the socio-economic and cultural milieu of the society. The human rights groups, environment protection and conservation groups and women and child welfare movements are already making their voices heard across the country. While the number of non-governmental organizations continues to swell further, these have helped to solve the problem of unemployment by providing part-time or full time use of the skills and surplus manpower.

One of the remarkable phenomenon spurring the growth of civil society is symbolized by the NGO movement has been the exposure of Nepalese people to the multi-media environment. If the waiver of the restrictive clause of cancellation of registration and seizure of newspapers has promoted increased investment of private entrepreneurs in the print media industry including newspapers, the lowering cost of dish antennae and ready access to numerous regional and international channels has created an open information environment unpredicted before. From the yardstick of press the most liberal and free country in South Asia. It is a country, which provides unrestricted entry and dissemination of information materials including newspapers, a case without any parallel in other SAARC nations. With all the attributes of a free and liberal democratic environment, the information systems of Nepal are increasingly emerging as an important factor in shaping the course of civil society movements.

But potentialities apart, mass media sector in Nepal is baffled by numerous difficulties and contradictions which act as inhibiting factors in the evolution of information saturated dynamic social structure, strong enough to sustain and nurture the newly established freedom and democratic society.

7

PAKISTAN

A Making of Meaning: The Transdisciplinary Women's Studies Conference — ASR/Institute of Women's Studies Lahore

Background

Women's studies as a discipline is not well established in Pakistan even within academic circles. This reflects the strongly patriarchal nature of Pakistan's society and the limited availability of education for women and girls. Women's groups and nongovernment organizations (NGOs) work to improve conditions for women but do not always have access to the theoretical tools of analysis.

The interdisciplinary and multidimensional nature of women's studies, both in theory and in practice, can often mean that the area suffers from misconceptions, an absence of a shared framework, and the isolation of scholars and others working on the subject matter.

In order to strengthen interconnections and to promote an inclusive approach, a transdisciplinary women's studies conference was organized to build links among scholars, organizations, writers, artists, and activists working in the field and to enhance intersections between theory, practice, culture, and social change. In so doing the organizers hoped to reduce the fragmentation of many women's studies initiatives and their restriction to the social sciences. ASR/ Institute of Women's Studies Lahore (IWSL) is involved in a variety of academic and activist pursuits including community work, assisting theater and arts groups, producing films, and conducting academic courses. It established IWSL, and held the first women's studies conference in Pakistan.

It also established the first feminist press in Pakistan. IWSL is committed to promoting connections between theory and practice in its work and understands that rigorous academic training can inform the ways social justice is sought. Knowledge is seen to have an important role in the transformation of both individuals and societies, thus the conference was proposed as a way to share and create new knowledge, to promote awareness of women's issues, and to bring together women in various disciplines and fields of activity.

Objectives and Scope

The conference title reflects its objectives:

- to explore and expand the understanding of women's studies by bringing together Pakistani and other South Asian women working on national issues, policy, literature, activism, and cultural expression
- to bring together Pakistani and South Asian women working in different fields and disciplines to reduce the isolation of scholars in women's studies and the fragmentation of knowledge
- to develop networking among the participants and to establish networks between conference participants and IWSL

IWSL invited participants from Pakistan as well as from France, South Asia, and the United States. The inclusion of international participants promoted collaboration on human rights issues and concerns, many of which are shared throughout the region. All participants were active in promoting the cause of women through activism, scholarship, or creative expression. As many participants were new to the field, the conference played an important role in establishing frameworks and networks, particularly for the many younger attendees.

The conference was multidisciplinary and multimedia. Along with formal presentations and poetry and prose readings, there were performances by dancers, an art exhibition, video and film screenings, and a magazine launch. Music also played an important part with conference organizers initiating the involvement of participants in songs and dancing throughout the conference. IWSL staff were very attentive to the comfort of participants and ensured that good communication and positive experiences strengthened the networks formed over the 5 days of the conference.

In line with the commitment to bringing together women working in diverse fields and to highlight the intersections between theory, activism, and artistic expression, the conference was organized around four main themes:

The women's movement addressed the forms of resistance women in Pakistan and South Asia have taken, the issues around which they have mobilized, and forms of organization and their functioning. The relationship between the women's movement and other forms of social struggle was also discussed

The theme of women and literature was included to highlight the importance of women's writing in the women's movement and the place of literature in raising women's issues. Isolation of women writers was identified as a particular problem, and the conference offered a space for them to meet, share ideas, and gain strength from shared experiences3 The politics of identity and ideology dealt with concerns over the role of the state, nation, and religious institutions in circumscribing opportunities for women by defining their positions and determining their identities. The conference explored the process, implications, and impact of nationalist and religious ideologies

Presentations in the area of women and development encompassed questions of the impact of development on women and a broad range of topics including economics, politics, the environment, land, housing, health, and education. They aimed to promote discussion of alternative development models based on the needs and aspirations of the majority of Pakistani people

Project Outcomes

The conference was extremely successful in terms of achieving its objectives. The careful planning and preparation of the event, the enthusiasm of IWSL staff, the varied and stimulating program, and the participation of delegates and the audience all contributed to its success. The discussion of conference papers and presentations was lively and engaged, and the cultural presentations were well received. Participants discussed issues at meals and social events and interacted with IWSL staff. Thus the objectives of developing networking among participants and between participants and IWSL staff were easily met. The varied program brought together people working in different areas who were pleased to find they shared concerns and approaches with other participants.

The wider public attended the poetry and prose readings further enhancing the reach of this network. The public readings served to further publicize the work of IWSL, to spread understanding of women's studies, and to promote the work of the female writers. The importance of cultural forms of expression of women's experiences and understanding was evident in enthusiastic responses to the dance, film, video, and visual arts presentations.

The objectives were further achieved by the high level of publicity the conference attracted. The conference was reported in newspapers and magazines for several days running. The poetry and prose readings were well publicized, and an ongoing debate was initiated between local columnist Hussain Haqani and conference delegate Anis Haroon. This debate continued to make headlines for a month. Thus the profile of women's studies was raised significantly in Pakistan, and many important conference topics and events gained the attention of the media. Most of the papers presented at the conference are being published by IWSL. This will achieve the aim of promoting women's studies and of continuing to establish and reinforce dialogue among women working in diverse fields. The publication will also help new scholars, activists, and artists to identify contacts and to learn from others working for women's rights.

The long-term benefits of the conference are evidenced in the publications, the new networks, and the establishment of workshops and seminars by participants based on the themes of the conference. The conference has established and nurtured the health of the women's movement in Pakistan and has emphasized the importance of dialogue, debate, and rigorous scholarship that is socially and politically responsible.

TRAINING PROGRAM FOR WOMEN ARTISANS - HAWWA ASSOCIATES

Background

Significant numbers of women in Pakistan are engaged in handicraft and tailoring activities including, for example, up to 30-40% of women in the North West Frontier Province

(NWFP). In poor households especially, female artisans can be important economic providers. Unfortunately, their economic contributions have not translated into a higher socioeconomic status. Poor women's human development indices in Pakistan are very low even by developing country standards. Inequalities between women and men and boys and girls are seen in every aspect of life. Despite some improvement in women's status in the last 30 years, the position of indigent women in Pakistan remains dismal. Pakistan's poor position internationally is seen in the United Nations Development Programme's Gender-related Development Index (GDI) 2000, where the country currently ranks 135 out of 174. On the Gender Empowerment Measurement (GEM) 1999, Pakistan ranked 100 out of the 102 countries measured. Such gender disparities are aggravated by the remoteness of many rural villages and the strict observation of purdah in more rural and isolated areas.

There is an urgent need to improve the socioeconomic status of poor female artisans as one strategy for improving the socioeconomic status of poor women in general, yet there are major barriers to the development of handicrafts as a form of income generation.

- Female artisans typically work at home where they must juggle production with household responsibilities
- They often lack confidence due to their lack of education and resources
- They lack experience outside the home due to gender segregation, restricted mobility, and the prevailing belief that men represent the household in public
- Poor female artisans often have no access to credit with which to buy new materials or to increase their production

- They tend to reproduce traditional patterns and color schemes familiar in their local communities and have little understanding of product development and changing market conditions
- Given their general isolation from other female artisans, markets, and craft networks, they are easily exploited by middlemen and women who pay them very low prices for their work

Hawwa Associates has been addressing the needs of poor female artisans in Pakistan for 20 years. From their Craft Sale Cooperative in Islamabad, they have provided craft training, sales and marketing advice, gender awareness training, and market links. Hawwa's limited resources have, however, made it difficult to deliver craft training, capacity building, and market links to female artisans in more remote parts of Pakistan such as NWFP and Balauchistan Province. With Asian Development Bank funding, Hawwa was able to strengthen regional and national links among female artisans through a series of training workshops held in Dera Ismail Khan (NWFP), Quetta (Balauchistan) and Hyderabad (Sindh).

Objectives and Scope

The project comprised three workshops, one each in Hyderabad, Dera Ismail Khan (D.I.K.) and Quetta, to train 90 women in craft making. The objectives were the following:

- to develop the concept of self-help groups as a mechanism for strengthening women's confidence and to deliver capacity training in areas such as business and marketing skills
- to encourage the adoption of new product designs in line with more marketable styles and colors while drawing on women's existing skills and knowledge of traditional styles

- to strengthen national links with nongovernment organizations (NGOs) and market networks, including market links with Hawwa Craft Cooperatives as an alternative sales outlet
- to raise awareness of the legal and social rights of women in Pakistan
- to identify regional/provincial craft styles for documentation and study visits

Prior to the workshops, Hawwa visited each area in order to survey the various craft styles and to identify potential workshop participants. Artisans were asked to prepare products for sale and display and, where receptive, to also prepare products in new designs, shapes, and colors. The training coordinator of Hawwa advised interested women on popular types of cloth, embroidery threads, and designs drawing on her knowledge of Pakistan's urban markets. In addition, she consulted with designers and fashion experts on her return for their advice on how to remodel traditional cross-stitch designs and colors from D.I.K. and Quetta.

The challenge to conduct pre-training visits and deliver such training to all three areas was considerable requiring prior consultation with men in the different communities in order to get their permission for women from their communities or families to be involved. In the case of Balauchistan, six men were allowed to sit in as observers so the women from their families could participate in the training.

Outcomes

The three training workshops attracted a range of female artisans including the following:

- women who wanted to begin to sell their products but lacked confidence, know how, and/or connections

- individual micro-entrepreneurs interested in Hawwa as an alternative sales outlet to shopkeepers and middlemen/women
- members of an existing self-help group who lacked business and marketing skills
- Highly skilled artisans seeking innovative approaches to product design and operational support

There was very good feedback from all participants on the content of training which covered topics such as female entrepreneurs, selection of materials, design, quality control, basics of finished products, pricing, billing, budgeting, credit and savings, marketing, and women's legal and social rights. Significant outcomes were achieved in this project from both an economic and empowerment perspective.

Economic Value

The following occurred as a result of training.

A number of women have formed self-help groups based on proximity and craft type in order to facilitate sales and marketing. For example, female embroiders and basket weavers from D.I.K. formed a total of five self-help groups. Representatives of these groups visit Hawwa every 3 months for further craft training

A number of women have opened bank accounts or have accessed loans. For example, 3% of the workshop participants at D.I.K. opened a bank account to organize earnings and savings. Twenty percent of participants from D.K.I. have taken out loans from the Agricultural Bank/Khushhali Bank or from the First Women's Bank. The First Women's Bank in Quetta has committed to lending up to Rs.10,000 to women in semi-urban areas

Thirty-four women from the three areas are sending consignments to Hawwa Craft Cooperatives in Islamabad.

Seventeen women from Hyderabad area are each earning between Rs.1500 and 3000 per month from this transaction. The three embroidery groups send items once a month to Hawwa's cooperative in Islamabad through male family members who collect sales advice and cash for any items sold that month

Home-based entrepreneurship has expanded and multiplied in all sectors. Following the successful relationship between Hyderabad and Hawwa, other NGOs in Sindh are developing craft and home-based income generating projects for women. In Balauchistan, the Directorate of Social Welfare made a commitment to establish a craft center for women

Women are keen to adopt new materials, colors, and designs as they recognize the value of producing goods attractive to consumers. Craft styles that have been modified in line with market needs include modifying the traditional colors of D.I.K. cross stitching; production of Balauchi embroidery as wall hangings, cushion covers, and evening bags; and adopting Ralli work (native to Sindh) for dress designs

Female artisans who supply Hawwa are keen to receive its on-going written advice on style, color, shape, and number

Women's Empowerment

The issue of women's empowerment was at the heart of this project. Workshop participants raised related issues spontaneously, particularly in the context of tribal or patriarchal attitudes that constrained women's craft work. Women in Quetta, for example, said that the major obstacle to their economic development was the perception that craft work was a supplementary form of income to be fitted around a woman's primary responsibilities, that is, household duties. This attitude informed shopkeepers and middlemen who used it to justify paying very low wages in installments.

The project had some beneficial outcomes with respect to women's empowerment.

Some men have begun to see women's economic activities in a new light. This is reflected by the support of male family members who take consignments to the Hawwa Cooperative in Islamabad

The formation of self-help groups, craft networks, and other structures of support during the project helped women develop confidence and a stronger sense of themselves as entrepreneurs

Women used the workshops to discuss their anger and frustration with existing gender relations. This heightened their desire to be rid of certain local customs and spurred them to champion other sociopolitical issues.

GIRLS' EDUCATION PROJECT

Background

Girls' educational attainment in Pakistan continues to lag behind the level of education attained by boys. This is seen in literacy levels and school enrollment figures, which reveal that large numbers of girls have limited access to even basic schooling. For example, the primary school enrollment rate for girls in 1996-1997 was estimated to be 66 percent of the total female population, compared to 90.7 percent of boys. At middle school, the rate was 37 percent for girls and 64 percent for boys. There are also significant provincial and rural disparities, with only three percent of rural 12-year old girls continuing at school, compared to 18 percent of boys. For example women's literacy rates are lowest in the North West Frontier Province (NWFP) and Balochistan. Literacy figures for 1995, show that only 12 percent and 6.6 percent of women in the NWFP and in Balochistan respectively were literate, compared to over 47 percent and 25 percent of men in these provinces.

There are many social and cultural reasons for this imbalance including poverty, early marriages of girls, cultural attitudes towards female education, restrictions on female mobility and gender discrimination in the household. Girls frequently drop out of school to stay at home to help with household chores and look after younger siblings. Many families view the formal education of girls as a waste of family resources and give priority to educating sons. Early marriage of girls also works against girls continuing at school. Other structural factors include the lack of female teachers and schools for girls in rural areas, distance of schools from villages and poor quality of teaching. As a result, the educational facilities and resources allocated to girls persistently fall behind those given to boys.

Khwendo Kor (or Sisters' Home) has been trying to break the silence surrounding such gender inequality by mobilizing community support for girls' education and advocating for policy reform. Registered in 1993, Khwendo Kor is a non-profit, non-government organization striving for the social and economic development of women and children under six main program areas: social organization; community-based education for women and girls; primary health care; women's microenterprise development; human and institutional development; and advocacy.

Under its community-based education program, Khwendo Kor has successfully established 100 community schools throughout NWFP. In the district of Dir for example, Khwendo Kor has established 37 community-based schools, with a total of 47 teachers and 1448 girls and 55 boy students. To support these schools and to encourage parents to take an active role in their children's education, Khwendo Kor has also established Parent Teachers Associations and Village Education Committees in these communities.

Despite its successes at the community-level, Khwendo Kor - in common with other small NGOs - has difficulty reaching and influencing government leaders and policy makers. This restricts the range of advocacy work that such organizations can achieve. To overcome such limitations, Khwendo Kor sought support from ADB and RETA 5889 to develop its institutional capacity in the area of advocacy and to strengthen its leverage at government and policy levels in order to promote girls' education in the North West Frontier Province.

Components

Project components include:

- To create an enabling environment for girls' education.
- To establish a provisional and divisional level education network.
- To increase social pressure to bring about positive change in education policy.
- To develop a database of organizations and institutions working on girls' education.
- To stimulate informed debate and public consultation on girls' education.
- To promote girls' education through publications and the media.

The duration of the project is 12 months. The project has three main components to support the above objectives:

- A provincial seminar on girls' education.
- To publish a quarterly newsletter and contribute articles on girls' education to local and national press, and

- To develop an Education Resource Centre at Khwendo Kor offices.

A provincial-level Education Core Group (ECG), comprising of representatives from NGOs, CBOs and government departments, was first established in 1996. Due to a lack of funds, however, it had not been functional for over two years. Funding through RETA 5889 has enabled the ECG to be re-established, with Khwendo Kor acting as convenor. Membership is growing as organizations involved in education all over the North West Frontier Province are contacted and invited to join. Over the course of the project, a number of divisional workshops will be held for members. The purpose of these workshops is to share information on the constraints and opportunities in the area of girls' education. Issues, relevant experiences and positive developments discussed in these workshops will be shared to others through a quarterly newsletter and other media outlets.

A provincial-level seminar on girls' education will be held following the establishment of the ECG and the conclusion of the divisional workshops. Participants in the seminar will include NGOs, CBOs, ECG members, academics, donor agencies, media and government representatives. The aim of this seminar is to promote the role of the ECG in education policy and review, as well as to establish the ECG as an important forum for addressing key issues concerning girls' education.

The quarterly newsletter established under the project is important as it will strengthen information sharing between ECG members and the advocacy role of Khwendo Kor. To support this initiative, a full-time consultant has been hired to establish the proposed Urdu-language newsletter. The newsletter will include articles on girls' education, field experiences, research findings and analysis of new government policy, strategies and press clippings. The Education Resource Centre not only supports current project components, but also provides an important basis for future advocacy in the area of girls' education. The Centre is open to individual researchers, academic institutions as well as government and non-government organizations, and has already started to build a collection of books, reports, case studies, audio and video materials, policy documents and newspaper clippings related to girls' education.

Outcomes

Several divisional workshops have been held to date, resulting in a growing network of NGO and CBO representatives wishing to join the ECG. These workshops have also provided an important forum for sharing information on the constraints and opportunities relating to girls' education in the different regions. A summary of small group discussions held at a divisional workshop in D.I. Khan in NWFP is presented below.

The establishment of the ECG is well underway with Khwendo Kor refining the terms of reference for members. Following discussions with ADB's GAD Specialist, Khwendo Kor is proposing to establish an Executive within the ECG to act as a Sector Support Group to the provincial government. The Executive would be limited to between 10 and 12 elected members and a small number of honorary positions (such as the provincial Director General and Secretary of Education). Selection criteria for elected members would include experience in the field of education for at least three years, policy experience in the area of girls' education, and advocacy skills. This would facilitate contact with the government, which to date has been reluctant to be involved in ECG activities including the district workshops.

As a result of district workshops and information sharing on the constraints facing girls' education, Khwendo Kor in consultation with ADB's GAD Specialist have drafted Action Plans in regard to two critical issues. Firstly, Khwendo Kor in common with other ECG members has witnessed a growing trend amongst reactionary religious groups to criticize girls' education, including their enrollment in community-based schools. To deflect such comments, Khwendo Kor and the ECG will develop and disseminate strategies that mobilize community support for schools and the education of girls. This has already been done to great effect in a few areas where village leaders have informed local religious leader not to interfere in the general affairs of the village and used cultural values - such as the value of literacy and a respect for education - to discredit religious leaders' arguments. Other strategies include holding community consultations on the value of educating girls, and involving mothers in such discussions as they are often more supportive of their daughters' education.

Secondly, Khwendo Kor and other organizations involved in establishing community schools are to propose that the Education Department assume financial responsibility for community-based schools established by the NGO and CBO sector after five years of operation. They also want the Education Department to administer examinations and certificates to students of such schools, who are currently disadvantaged by the lack of formal recognition of their schooling. Furthermore, Khwendo Kor and the ECG would like the Education Department to consider mechanisms similar to those implemented in community schools to encourage girls enrollment, such as:

- Encouraging high levels of community participation and support,
- Locating schools in close proximity to villages,

- Providing low cost education to girls,
- Inviting mothers to actively participate in Parent Teacher Associations and Village Education Committees, and
- Focusing on re-enrollment of girl school dropouts by funding limited places for these students.
- Summary of Small Group Discussions, Divisional Workshop in D.I. Khan, NWFP.

Key Constraints to Girls' Education

Economic

- Poverty, unemployment and the cost of education. When resources are limited families choose to invest in their sons' education.
- Child labor within families, particular the use of daughters to assist with domestic chores and child minding.
- Families reluctant to invest in education as it does not seem to guarantee future work or a more high paying job in man rural areas.

Social

- The practice of early marriage.
- Educated girls seen as more likely to break away from 'tradition' and to challenge father's and husband's authority.
- Distance of schools from home and restricted mobility of girls.
- Families reluctant to encourage girls to leave home for further education or more skilled work.
- Education and work not seen as priorities for girls, in contrast to marriage and motherhood.

- Religious groups which mobilize followers against schools on the basis of the lack of segregation between boys and girls; the lack of female teachers; and the presumed moral dangers of educating girls.

Administrative

- No education budget as the Annual Development Program for Education at the provincial level has been frozen for the past seven years.
- Education is not seen as a priority by the government, resulting in no facilities, few schools and high teacher:student ratios. In this context, many parents see school fees paid for daughters as a waste of money.
- Low quality of teachers, teaching resources and facilities, compounded by high levels of teacher absenteeism.
- Lack of female teachers is due to isolation, lack of transportation and low salary. These also result in high levels of absenteeism among female teachers.
- New schools must be built on land provided by the community free of charge. This results in schools being built some distance away from villages thus increasing the risks for female teachers and students.

Future Direction

Building capacity in the area of advocacy cannot be achieved in the short term. Effective advocacy requires long-term networking and relationship building across a range of relevant government departments and non-government organizations. While Khwendo Kor has made a start in this area, there is scope to establish contact with other government agencies, particularly women-oriented agencies such as the Women's Development Department

(WDD) and the National Commission on the Status of Women. In terms of relationship building, Khwendo Kor and the ECG could offer support to these government agencies similar to the role of Sector Support Group it plans to offer to the provincial Education Department. The ECG should also consider inviting the Secretary of WDD to become a member of the ECG Executive. ADB can foster such linkages through its Capacity Building Project on Gender and Governance, which involves both the National Commission on the Status of Women and the Secretary, Women's Development Department.

The critical link between literacy, education and economic growth needs to be better supported by the government. This is in line with ADB's Pakistan Country Strategy Program (2002-2004), which highlights economic growth and human development, including education, literacy and GAD as thematic priority areas. The CSP also targets GAD as one of three priority areas for technical assistance and supports the general thrust of the government's Poverty Reduction Strategy Paper (2001). Building on this, ADB may want to consider supporting specific gender components in all education sector program loans and technical assistance. For example, projects such as Primary School Quality Sector Development Project (formerly, Teachers' Training and Primary School Quality Project) have opportunities to include training components that encourage the retention of girls throughout primary and into secondary school.

PLANT NURSERY PROJECT IN MALIWAL VILLAGE — SHIRKAT GAH

"When I first started working in the nursery, my in-laws were very upset and thought I was going out for no reason. On coming home, they would often scold me saying, 'Madam has come back after roaming about here and there.' Now that I am able to financially contribute to the family, their attitude has changed completely and now they admire my work." (working committee member)

"In the beginning we knew nothing about raising plants in polythene bags, shifting, or grafting and did not even know the names of these ornamental plants. But now we have learnt everything and people are surprised that we now know the English names of plants." (working committee members)

"In the past my husband used to beat me. I didn't say anything because he was the one providing for the family. After my involvement with Swani Sanjh and earning money from the nursery, I have realized that he is not justified in beating me." (working committee member)

"I used to be very shy. I was so shy that I couldn't go out of the house in new clothes. Now I go out confidently and can even bargain with shopkeepers." (working committee member)

"We know a time will come when no further financial support will be available for the plant nursery, but we are determined to make it take off, and we will work harder and continue our efforts for marketing our plants." (management committee member)

Background

In Pakistan, women's important economic contributions are often unacknowledged and hidden within their household work. Social and cultural norms such as the institution of purdah reinforce the view that a woman's legitimate place is in the home firmly under the control of her husband or family.

Such norms underplay women's roles as important farm and household producers and constrain their capacities to act as independent economic producers.

Poor farming households in Pakistan have limited access to agricultural extension services, credit facilities, new plant varieties, and equipment. Women from such households are further marginalized typically having no access to credit and agricultural services in their own rights. Gender disparities in literacy rates, education, and economic resources conspire with sociocultural practices such as female segregation and restricted mobility to deprive poor women of access to such services.

Nonetheless, women's socioeconomic development in Pakistan is ultimately dependent on their ability to pursue economic opportunities that not only contribute to the economic wellbeing of their families but also-and importantly - give women greater control over their own lives. One women's nongovernment organization (NGO) that has been working in this area is Shirkat Gah. This NGO is committed to assisting poor women develop sustainable livelihoods through the development of innovative agricultural products. In working towards this goal, Shirkat Gah recognizes the need to provide a supportive framework in which women can gain self-reliance and self-confidence as well as learn new technical skills.

With funding from the Asian Development Bank, Shirkat Gah has been able to continue the development of its plant nursery project in the small Punjabi village of Maliwal. Shirkat Gah is collaborating with the community-based women's group Swani Sanjh to establish an ornamental plant commercial nursery as an income generating project for village women.

Objectives and Scope

The objective of the project was to establish an economically viable and operational commercial nursery to:

- enhance the income level of local women

- facilitate local women to develop and strengthen market links
- establish the plant nursery as a self-sustaining income generating activity

The project compromised the following activities:

- purchase of nursery plants, seedlings, and other stock
- construction of bamboo sheds, hand trolleys, iron gates, and other infrastructure
- establishment and capacity building of a committee responsible for managing the nursery on a day-to-day basis including the marketing of plants and record keeping
- establishment and training of a working committee responsible for running and maintaining the nursery, including preparing the plants, potting, weeding, pruning, and watering
- recruitment of a marketing consultant to assist in the selection of high-value plants and to provide advice on market links

Technical Skills and Capacity Building

The management and working committees were given a range of training and capacity-building exercises.

Members of the management committee were given training in record keeping and bookkeeping at Shirkat Gah

Members of the working committee were given training in the care and maintenance of plants such as potting, grafting, watering, pruning, and so on

All members benefited from the knowledge they learned from the gardener/marketing consultant recruited during the project. He identified plants of high sale value and established market links for the sale and purchase of plants.

He also trained the working committee in the stages at which different plants and seedlings need to be purchased for the nursery

Several visits by the management and working committees were made to Pattoki and other nearby towns to develop market links. Shirkat Gah also sponsored a trip to Lahore for the women to visit a number of plant nurseries

Members of the management committee made several exposure visits in order to develop their understanding of market-related agricultural activities and to interact with members of similar village-based enterprises. On one exposure visit, the management committee made a formal presentation to over 500 participants, comprising male and female small farmers as well as representatives of local community-based organizations, NGOs, and government departments

Outcomes

As a result of the project, an area of 1250 square feet was laid out into a plant nursery complete with green sheds, beds for growing plants, and water channels. The nursery has a capacity for growing more than 10,000 plants and saplings. The income from the nursery has been steady. Although small in volume, to the women involved in the nursery, this income has made a significant difference to their households and to their status as economic contributors.

Women's Empowerment

Women not only developed an income generating activity through their involvement in the plant nursery, they also acquired new technical and business skills and gained confidence and greater control over their lives. The comments above reveal the extent to which these positive outcomes developed over the project. Other outcomes include the following.

- The women members of Swani Sanjh now operate, manage, and conduct market-related activities entirely on their own.
- Women of the working committee make decisions related to sales, purchasing, price negotiations, and promotional activities independently.
- This success has attracted other women to join Swani Sanjh resulting in 36 new members over the project period.

As a consequence, men and women of the community now see women's potential to manage and operate a nursery.

- The male gardeners who initially gave training to the women were of the opinion that women would not be able to run a nursery. Their attitude was discouraging to say the least. Very quickly they realized that women have the ability to learn new skills and the capacity to run this type of business.
- Landowners of nearby villages have invited the working committee to hold orientation sessions for women in their villages about setting up plant nurseries.
- Local residents now buy plants from the local nursery and the general interest in ornamental plants has increased.
- One member of Swani Sanjh has decided to lease one or two canal of land on her own in order to grow roses for ubtan (a beauty paste).
- Another villager has requested the working committee to train his son in gardening. Some families have been motivated to explore other market opportunities such producing and marketing vegetables.

BURN CARE PROJECT, WATAN WELFARE SOCIETY

Background

The treatment of burns is arguably one of the most expensive and specialized of medical treatments. Burns care requires the combination of a number of surgical and general medical skills, such as pediatrics, plastic surgery, infection control, palliative care and labor intensive critical care nursing. On top of this, burn victims need intensive, one-on-one treatment from allied health professionals such as physiotherapists, psychiatrists and psychologists.

The irony is that countries with the greatest need often lack the facilities to treat and rehabilitate burn victims. Pakistan is one such country. For example, there is no publicly-funded specialized burn center or hospital burn unit in Pakistan. The only purpose-built burn unit in the country is the Army Burn Centre in Kharion, and this hospital only accepts civilian burn victims who can afford the high fee charged.

While there are no official statistics on the types and causes of burns, figures collected by non-government organizations suggest an increasing occurrence of burns. The majority of burns are accidental and result from contact with gas stoves, lamps, leaking gas pipes, exposed electrical wiring, boiling water, hot oil, etc. Most burns occur in the home, in or around the kitchen.

As a result, women and children are most at risk of burns. According to data collated by the Watan Welfare Society, out of 306 burn victims treated at their Burns Care Centre between January 1999 and April 2000, women and children accounted for 82 percent of all victims. Of the total number, 62 percent of victims were burnt in or around the kitchen, with children most at risk here. Of the 41 cases of suicide treated by the Centre, 88 percent of suicide burn victims were women.

There is also disturbing evidence that increasing numbers of burn victims - particularly those described as suicide cases - are young women who have been set alight or had acid thrown on them by their husband or in-laws. Such extreme violence can be severely debilitating for women, who face ostracism because of their scarred appearance and loss of mobility. It is also a form of violence that is frequently covered up by the perpetrators as 'accidental.'

The Human Rights Commission of Pakistan reported that between 1998 and 1999, more than 560 cases of women were burnt in the home in Punjab (Pakistan's most populous state), and that while many of these cases where suspicious, there were only a handful of arrests.

The Progressive Women's Association tracked 3,560 women who were hospitalized after being attacked at home with fire, gasoline or acid between 1994 and 1995. Victims of such crimes face special problems in terms of their rehabilitation back into society.

Even in the case of accidental burns, women and girls are often rejected by their husbands, in-laws or seen as unmarriageable due to scars and in some cases their limited mobility. For these reasons, programs designed to treat burns must incorporate a wide range of specialist services, including education and prevention campaigns, specialist surgeons, counseling and rehabilitation. In particular, there is a need for the professionals involved to structure support services to meet the special needs of female victims.

Alarmed by the lack of specialist burn care available in Pakistan, the Watan Welfare Society established a Burn Care Centre in Peshawar in January 1999. The Centre has treated over 300 burn victims since 1999, drawing on the skills of a dedicated team of volunteer medical specialists and allied health professionals. The Burn Care Centre has

15 volunteer specialists, including medical officers, an anesthetist, a pediatric surgeon, plastic surgeons, an orthopedic surgeon, general physicians, a cardiologist, an ophthalmologist, a physiotherapist, psychiatrist, psychologist and microbiologist. In its 15-bed Burn Care Centre, the Watan Welfare Society provides heavily subsidized or free medical, nursing and allied health care depending on the victim's situation.

Lacking funds to fully outfit its laboratory and operating theater, as well the resources to promote awareness on the prevention and care of burn cases, Watan Welfare Society approached ADB for support under RETA 5889 for additional equipment and the conduct of an awareness program.

Components

The project's main objectives are to prevent the occurrence, and improve the treatment, of burn cases amongst women and children. To achieve these objectives, the project sought to promote awareness on the prevention and treatment of burns cases, as well as upgrade the curative facilities at the Burn Care Centre.

The project also hopes to make the Centre self sustaining. By funding new laboratory equipment, the Centre will be able to perform its own pathology tests and blood screenings, thus saving money and also providing an opportunity to make money by providing such services to private clinics, teaching hospital and other organizations in Peshawar for a fee.

Project components include:

- A one-day seminar on burns issues in Peshawar designed to build the awareness and capacity of government institutions (notably the police, health department), NGOs, CBOs, the media, medical students and young doctors;

- Upgrading of laboratory and curative facilities at the Burn Care Centre, including a micro laboratory machine, anesthesia machine, surgical instruments, monitor and pulse oxymeter; and,
- Production of brochures and pamphlets on prevention and care of burns.

Outcomes

The major outcome of the project has been the improved treatment and recovery rates experienced at the Centre after the purchase of the equipment. For example, the dermatones and mesher improve the rate of successful skin grafts as well as providing more sightly skin grafts. The cost of treatment has also decreased as procedures are more successful (thus avoiding the need to repeat surgery) and as the Burn Care Centre can meet its own pathology requirements. In terms of prevention and education, the seminar held in Peshawar was a great success. Although it was envisaged that about 150 people would attend, closer to 400 participants attended. A number of papers and discussion panel were held, with major topics covering:

- Cause and treatment of burn patients at the Burn Care Centre
- Non-accidental burns in children, and
- Suicide and incidental burns amongst women.

The seminar was important in raising awareness of the need to fund and promote specialist burns care to government and non government sector. Apart from such formal occasions, the Centre relies on its patients to promote awareness of such issues. As the Centre's Pediatrics Surgeon Dr Said Alam Mahasud commented- "we educate every patient". This is certainly true in the case of Saadia, a young lady health worker and former patient at the Centre.

However, efforts to promote prevention and treatment require brochures and posters to enable the dissemination of important information. For this reason, the Centre is producing material not only for seminar participants but also for people working at the grassroots level, such as social workers and lady health workers.

The Centre is currently considering how it might support a public campaign at the grassroots level by working cooperatively with such groups. One mechanism that has been trialed and found very successful is to run a Burns Camp. So far the Centre has held on burns camp in a rural area of the province.

The idea here is that staff from the Centre visit villages to provide curative and preventive services. This camp also helped to raise the profile of the Centre and is helping to contribute to the increasing number of women patients brought by their families to the Centre. Not only that, but with knowledge, there is a greater number of acute cases coming to the Centre directly (rather than from referral) and thus more timely. Such changes dramatically improve the burn victim's chances of survival and recovery.

Advocacy is also on the agenda and already members have met with government officials on the need for quality standards to regulate the manufacture of cooking equipment and consumer rights legislation to ensure such standards are respected. Other issues here include occupational health and safety regulations to protect and compensate workers burnt at work.

Finally, the project reached its objective in terms of sustainability. Currently, the Centre is able to meet its recurrent costs although it is largely reliant on the volunteer services of its specialists. Funds generated from patient fees or fees from use of their laboratory service cover the cost of treatment and the rent of the building. There are however financial constraints in terms of future expansion and further improvement. There are also limitations on the types of information and material that the Centre can fund. To assist here, the Centre has developed a Web site to provide data on the incidence and cause of burns treated in the Centre and other educational material. However, as the Burn Care Centre realizes, there is a need for a coordinated approach to burns care which will require some government commitment to burns as a public health issue.

The Story of a Burn Victim: Saadia

Saadia is a lady health worker who suffered third degree burns to her legs and arms as the result of a leaking gas cylinder in the kitchen. Her husband's family brought her to the Burns Centre about two weeks after the accident. The delay was due to the family's lack of knowledge about the Burn Centre.

Finally, a doctor told her maternal uncle about the Centre and she was admitted. By the time Saadia was admitted, her wounds were infected, making treatment difficult. She spent over two months in the Centre undergoing several skin grafts as a result of the infection. During her stay, Saadia's family had to pay only for her room (because they wanted her to have a private room) and medications.

Talking to Saadia six months after the accident, she expresses her gratitude to the Centre. As a lady health worker, she realizes just how fortunate she is. She often comes across other women burn victims. As she says, burns are part of women's everyday experience, and yet she finds that the majority of women - like herself - are very ignorant of the risks and treatments available. She notes that many women who suffer serious burns are not taken to hospital because their families cannot afford the treatment or do not value the women in their family. Women who are taken to hospital often fare little better as there are no facilities for burn victims and low standards of sterility result in many infection-related deaths.

As a result of her experience, Saadia is committed to educating women on the prevention and treatment of burns. She says that women in her district have very limited knowledge of burn prevention measures and simple treatments, such as rolling victims in a blanket or putting the victim in cold water.

They also do not realize the importance of seeking treatment as soon as possible. In her work, she discusses her own experience as a way of educating women on the dangers of burns and publicizing the work of the Burn Centre. She believes lady health care workers can play a special role as they mostly deal with women and children, the primary victims of burns. What is needed however are posters and information on the prevention and treatment of burns from the government, which she can distribute to the households and health centers in her district.

Future Direction

There is obvious scope to use this Burn Care Centre as a model for other potential burn centers in Pakistan. The close cooperation between different professionals in the treatment and prevention of burns is a useful demonstration of the team-based approach required in burn care. This cooperation between different professionals and burn patients also proved very useful in terms of education and prevention campaigns.

The experience of medical staff associated with the Centre also offers practical insights in the establishment of adequate burn care facilities within Pakistan. ADB should consider the following minimum requirements recommended by Dr Said Alam Mahasud on behalf of Watan Welfare Society in future public and women's health projects:

- Financial allocation for a 10-15 bed burn unit for every one million of population in Pakistan; of a 5-10 bed burn intensive care unit for every twenty million of population in Pakistan;
- Establishment of one rehabilitation unit in each province;
- Establishment of at least one center of excellence for burn victims;
- A state-sponsored preventive campaign in print and electronic media to decrease the incidence of burns and crimes of violence against women;
- Legislation on quality control of public utilities (particularly gas and electricity supply) and the manufacture of domestic appliances; and,
- Penalty for negligence of public sector officials, public and private manufacturers who supply sub-standard services and goods.

The concern with women's health, public health and violence against women integral to the prevention and treatment of burns is in line with ADB's own priority areas of Human Development and Gender and Development as noted in the Country Strategy Program (2002-2004). ADB-financed loan projects in the areas of public health and women's health can build on this project by including specific components on the treatment and prevention of burns, allocating funding for the establishment of specialized burns treatment centers in public hospitals; and incorporating burns awareness and prevention campaigns in all public health and women's health projects. Lady health workers and other community-based health workers could be trained to deliver information on ways to reduce home-based accidental burns and first aid treatment of burn victims. Such information could be supported by mass awareness campaigns in the electronic and print media.

Technical assistance should also be provided to finance much needed research into the causes and extent of burn injuries in Pakistan. In particular, there is a need for research on the extent and nature of burn-related violence against women in order to design appropriate responses from the government and the community. This issue needs to be brought into the full glare of public scrutiny so that police and other government agencies are forced to address burn-related violence against women. ADB can assist here by including a component on burn-related violence in ADB-funded loan projects focusing on women's rights, women's health and violence against women in Pakistan. The National Commission on the Status of Women and the Ministry of Women's Development could be considered as appropriate executing agencies here.

Finally, ADB-funded projects in the area of legal reform and governance could investigate the area of standards and consumer protection. Standards - supported by penalties and compensation in the case of negligence - need to be established to cover the supply and maintenance of public utilities, such as gas and electricity, as well as the manufacture of household equipment such as stoves, gas cylinders and lights. Such issues could be included in relevant technical assistance projects, such as the Strengthening of Institutional Capacity for Judicial and Legal Reform and the proposed ADF-funded Judicial and Legal Reform Program There is also a need for well-enforced workplace occupational health and safety regulations to protect workers from negligence.

WOMEN'S LEGAL LITERACY — THE ASSOCIATION OF WOMEN OF SCIENCE TAJIKISTAN

Background of the Project

Enhancing women's legal literacy is crucial so that women can defend and further their rights and opportunities in all areas of social, political, and economic life. As in many countries, women in Tajikistan have very low levels of legal literacy and are unaware of their rights. A UNESCO study found that 94% of women in the sample with tertiary educations could not name any international document or law on the rights of women, and only 22% were familiar with national laws or constitutional guarantees regarding women's rights. The level of legal literacy among rural, less-educated women is even lower. Although non-discriminatory legislation for women is guaranteed by the country's constitution, in practice violations of women's rights are an everyday occurrence. One of the factors sustaining these violations is a general lack of awareness of women's rights.

Objectives and Scope

The Association of Women of Science Tajikistan (AWST) has long been involved in advocating women's rights, particularly in relation to violence against women. The main objective of this project was to raise rural women's legal literacy through a series of workshops and publications. Women's legal education was to be delivered through the following activities:

- acquainting women with basic international legal documents and national legislation concerning their rights
- determining the influence of violence and conflict on the moral and physical wellbeing of women
- identifying key causes of gender-based conflict and violence in order to develop mechanisms to reduce them
- training women in basic conflict resolution techniques

In all, eight women from AWST were involved in the project: two lawyers, one psychologist, one sociologist, and three local specialists (one each from the three regions).

Outcomes

The project was very successful and resulted in a number of positive outcomes in the areas of legal education, publications, and basic research into the status and violation of women's rights in Tajikistan.

In total, 90 women received legal education in Kofarnikhon, Kurgan-Tube, and Tursun-Zade. These 3-day workshops covered the following topics (dedicating one day to each): legal aspects of conflict resolution, women's rights in the family, and women's reproductive rights. At the end of each workshop, support groups were formed among the women in order to take the legal education program to the local level. Women were provided with packages of key international and national legislation relating to their rights including the Universal Declaration of Human Rights (1948), the UN Convention on Elimination of All Forms of Discrimination Against Women (CEDAW, 1979), the UN Declaration on Ending All Forms of Violence Against Women (1993), the Constitution of the Republic of Tajikistan, the criminal code, the family code (1998), the civil code (1999) and the labor code (1999).

During these workshops, women participated in a number of small group exercises designed to assist them to relate their internationally and constitutionally guaranteed rights to their everyday experiences at home and work. For example, following a session on CEDAW and the UN Declaration on Ending All Forms of Violence Against Women, participants were asked to "create" a set of laws to protect the rights of women in marriage and in the family. They were asked to consider issues such as whether women and men should have equal rights concerning children, whether domestic violence should be treated as a criminal offence, if there should be equal distribution of household work including child care, and who should decide the number of children in a family. This "legislation" was then compared to existing rights guaranteed in both international conventions and national legislation.

AWST also prepared a number of publications that were distributed to workshop participants among others. These included three pamphlets ('Violence: Is it possible to avoid?" "Sexual Violence and the Rights of Girls," and "Ethics of Sexual Relations and the Moral-Legal Responsibility of Youth") as well as two booklets ("How to Exit from Conflict" and "What about Conflict?").

Sociological research into women's legal literacy was also conducted during the project. In total, 450 women from Kofarnikhon, Kurgan-Tube, and Tursun-Zade completed a questionnaire focussing on women's legal literacy. Women were asked a series of questions relating to two key areas:

- their knowledge of international conventions, legislation, and other documents relating to women's rights
- their knowledge of national legislation and the constitutional provisions that pertain to women's rights

Overall, 83% were not familiar with any international document or law relating to women's rights. With respect to national laws and guarantees, only 23% knew that their country's constitution protects women's rights, and only 3.7% were familiar with any clauses relating to women's rights in the criminal and family codes. Based on this survey and on the comments of workshop participants, there is an urgent need to establish a system of women's legal education in Tajikistan. Legal education workshops conducted by women's nongovernment organizations are important avenues for women to learn about their rights and to gain the confidence to defend them when they are violated.

WOMEN'S CRISIS CENTERS — WOMEN'S PSYCHOLOGICAL REHABILITATION CENTRE

Background

Civil war and political conflict have disastrous long-term economic and social costs. The women and children of Tajikistan know this better than most. With 80% of the population below the poverty line, Tajikistan is among the world's 20 poorest nations. Tajikistan's 5-year conflict (1992-1997) left a legacy of 50,000 deaths, 600,000 displaced persons, 60,000 refugees, 55,000 orphans and 20,000 widows in a population of 5.8 million. The post-conflict period has not brought the expected prosperity. Paradoxically, life expectancy decreased after the war finished.

Tragically, gender-based violence against women and girls during the conflict has left a legacy of psychologically damaged women and men. Violence against women is endemic in Tajikistan and continues as an effect of post-conflict trauma and in response to continuing economic and social frustration. According to the Ministry of Health, about 70% of women who suffer depression live in a condition of acute or chronic family stress. Unfortunately, there is no system of free access to psychologists and other mental health specialists in the country. After 5 years of civil conflict and over a decade of economic transition following independence, Tajikistan's social sector is limping badly. In many rural areas it has collapsed. The majority of women cannot afford private consultations and consequently lack specialists' care and support in this area.

In affiliation with the Association of Women Scientists of Tajikistan (AWST), the Women's Psychological Rehabilitation Centre has worked to support Tajikistan's victims of violence, the majority of whom are women and girls. With funding from the Asian Development Bank, the centre sought to broaden and extend the reach of its services including establishing a telephone hotline in three women's crisis centers.

Objectives and Scope

Under the direction of the Women's Psychological Rehabilitation Centre in Dushanbe, the project aimed to strengthen, broaden, and extend the reach of services provided to women and teenagers at the centre and the three branch crisis centers in Kofarnikhon, Kurgan-Tube, and Tursun-Zade. The principle objective of the project was to rehabilitate injured women and teenagers through crisis centers' telephone hotlines and individual face-to-face consultations.

The following components were funded under this project:

- counseling and other assistance to victims of violence through a telephone hotline, individual face-to-face consultations, and referrals and consultations with professionals such as lawyers, psychologists, and gynecologists
- referrals and resources at the centers for the treatment and rehabilitation of female and child victims of violence
- education programs to raise the self-confidence and self-esteem of girls
- counseling and reproductive health and family planning services for teenagers through hot line telephone services and educational programs
- public educational activities including seminars, meetings, and training workshops

Outcomes

As a result of these activities, the following range of support and services was provided.

The telephone hotline assisted 900 women over a 12-month period. Sixty percent of the calls were from working married women ages 20-45 with children. Female callers displayed a number of psychological problems resulting from physical and psychological abuse including post-traumatic stress, depression, phobia, lack of self-esteem, and withdrawal from social activities.

An analysis of the calls revealed that 65% concerned psychological violence perpetrated by husbands, ex-husbands, or current partners; 48% related to domestic violence; 17% concerned physical violence against women; and 5% dealt with sexual violence.

Over 30% of the women experienced a complex mix of such abuse. In order to staff the telephone hotline, 15 women received 2 days of intensive training at each of the three branch crisis centers. In addition, hotline staff and other volunteers at each branch participated in an art therapy seminar designed to teach staff how to use drawing as a way of debriefing and managing the stress of their work.

Difficult or more complex cases were referred for individual consultation to various specialists including psychologists, psychotherapists, gynecologists, and lawyers. Many of these cases involved women who had been exposed to long-term domestic violence.

In addition, three support groups were established for female victims of violence. Each group worked together for 3 hours per week over a 3-month period. The majority of participants were victims of domestic violence with some the victims of sexual violence. Many women reported that due to their participation in these groups, they were able to recover their self-esteem and become socially active again.

Several educational programs were conducted during the project. Three seminars on the moral and sexual education of teenagers were conducted (one each in Kofarnikhon, Kurgan-Tube, and Tursun-Zade). Thirty young women and young men received training in the following areas: reproductive health, moral and legal education, cultural and ethical considerations, and the interrelationship between family and society. In addition, the crisis center devised three workshops entitled "You are not Alone," "A Life Free of Violence," and "Under the Protection of International Rights." These workshops were conducted in all three branches. A total of 90 participants attended in each branch including housewives, high school children, and social workers. All participants, including both young women and young men, found these workshops to be very informative.

"Women have rights and they can and must defend them!"

"I [now] understand that I have unfortunately been repeatedly exposed to violence in my life."

"I now understand that there is a lot of violence [in our society], and that I have the right to voice my objection both in my relations with my relatives and with men."

The project also resulted in four publications written by crisis centre staff. Two brochures were published: "Violence: Is it Possible to Avoid?" and "Methodological Recommendations on Work at the Crisis Centre. " In addition, two booklets were published: "Domestic Violence" and "Against Violence in the Family."

TRAINING UNEMPLOYED RURAL WOMEN BY BUSINESS WOMEN'S ASSOCIATION, TASHKENT OBLAST

Objectives

The aim of the project is to provide business education to women in 12 rural areas of Tashkent. Following the business training, women in the region will be able to (i) develop professional skills in finance and organising their own business; (ii) identify and carry out income-generating activities; (iii) improve socio-economic status.

Completion:

31 October 2001(The implementation period is 12 months)

Scope:

Each class consisted of 15 women. The course includes:

- Developing an Effective Business Plan
- Tax policy on Small and Medium Scale Businesses
- Starting a Small Business
- Legislation and Economic Rights

Project Implementation Results:

Major Outputs of the Project Include:

- Training sessions in 10 rayons were conducted;
- 181 rural women were trained;
- 72 women started their own small business;
- 73 new jobs were created;
- 7 women received loans from the local banks;
- 217 women were given consultation sessions on how to start their own small businesses.

The training programs were successful and there is a big demand for continuation of the program. The local Government gave a positive feedback. Four articles about the training were issued in the local newspaper.

The financial reports for the covered period were submitted to ADB. The Resident Mission Gender Specialist took part in the training in Bekabad and Pskent rayons in order to monitor the project implementation.

Integration of Gender Issues

This grant is clearly a women-targeted project, which calls for women's participation in the small entrepreneurship activity such as handicrafts, weaving and fancywork, sewing and tailoring, off-season vegetable and fruit production and new enterprises.

The understanding of gender as a crosscutting subject was developed from the very beginning.

Initially meetings were held in rayons of Tashkent Oblast with the Chairperson of BWA to brief training participants about the need for looking at gender issues in the project and the role of URM, GS in assisting the RETA. Emphasis was given on ADB's approach of mainstreaming gender in its projects. As a result of the above activities, a better understanding on GAD issues has been created within the project

Other Issues

Women participants emphasized that they need more training to increase their understanding of business promotion and marketing, money management and record-keeping, banking training for group leaders and management training. They also were unanimous in their desire for further skill development training for income generation.

Future requirements for group formation and training include:

(i) skill development training need to be associated with microcredit program

(ii) knowledge and skill for developing a cadre of new entrepreneurs to adopt off-farm microentrerprises

(iii) institutional strengthening of NGOs;

(iv) provide essential banking training to the NGOs staff;

There is considerable unmet demand among women for credit of the local banks for business expansion in small enterprises.

These women have difficulty meeting the complex requirements of the bank; There is a need to improve dissemination of entrepreneurial knowledge, especially among rural women, having a lack of experience and skills of managing small enterprises,

Findings

- Project was designed particularly to address gender considerations and improve the status of women;
- The local Government supports the BWA activities and welcomes the increasing number of new jobs created.
- Empowerment of women was confirmed by their involvement in business activities and social interactions with other group members and BWAs. They now actively participate in household matters in terms of financial contribution and decision-making process in the family;
- Project has provided benefits to families, particularly women, through the provision of improved access to the banks, property and business education;
- The BWA has enough training and technical capacity and staff to continue and replicate this project to another rayons in the country;

The RETA of this nature provides an opportunity to finance small NGOs such as BWAs at low cost, requiring minimal processing and ADB resources. At the same time, it generates an overall increase in ADB activities targeting women. It assists local institutions to develop their GAD capacity, and pilot-test new initiatives.

TRAINING OF WOMEN ENTREPRENEURS, BUSINESS WOMEN ASSOCIATION – BUKHARA OBLAST

Objectives

The project involves training of women-entrepreneurs. The specific objectives of the project are to:

(i) raise women's awareness of economic opportunities available to them;

(ii) build knowledge of women's legal rights;

(iii) create employment for women and their families;

(iv) facilitate interaction among women in order that they can co-operatively identify opportunities for women entrepreneurs.

It is expected that the training seminars will create a solid base for BWA to set up microcredit schemes for women entrepreneurs.

Completion

31 October 2001(The implementation period is 12 months)

Scope and Activity

Project activities include organising and carrying out training seminars, launching of an information campaign. BWA will analyse its experience in the project to learn lessons in enhancing women's entrepreneurial skills. As estimated 160 women entrepreneurs and their families will directly benefit from the improved ability of women to engage in income-earning activities. BWA will tap the women that were trained to establish women's microcredit co-operatives.

Project Implementation Results:

Major outputs of the training program are:

- Training sessions in 7 rayons were conducted;
- 157 rural women (more than originally expected) were trained;
- 68 women opened their own small business;
- 183 new jobs were created;
- 26 women received loans from the local bank;
- 17 women are in the process of getting loan from the local banks;
- 639 rural women were given a consultation sessions on how to start their small businesses.

Integration of Gender Issues:

This grant is clearly a women-targeted project, which calls for women's participation in the small entrepreneurship activity such as handicrafts, weaving and fancywork, sewing and tailoring, off-season vegetable and fruit production and new enterprises.

The understanding of gender as a crosscutting subject was developed from the very beginning. Initially meetings were held in rayons of Bukhara Oblast with the Chairperson of BWA to brief training participants about the need for looking at gender issues in the project. Emphasis was given on ADB's approach of mainstreaming gender in ADB-financed projects. As a result of the above activities, a better understanding on gender and development (GAD) issues has been created within the project.

Other Issues

- Women participants emphasized that they need more training to increase their understanding of business promotion and marketing, money management and record-keeping, banking training for group leaders and management training. They also were unanimous in their desire for further skill development training for income generation.

- Future requirements for group formation and training include:
  - (i) skill development training need to be associated with microcredit program
  - (ii) knowledge and skill for developing a cadre of new entrepreneurs to adopt off-farm microentrerprises
  - (iii) institutional strengthening of NGOs;
  - (iv) provide essential banking training to the NGOs staff;
- There is considerable unmet demand among women for credit of the local banks for business expansion in small enterprises. These women have difficulty meeting the complex requirements of bank;
- There is a need to improve dissemination of entrepreneurial knowledge, especially among rural women, having a lack of experience and skills of managing small enterprises;

Findings

- Project was designed particularly to address gender considerations and improve the status of women;
- The local Government supports the BWA activities and welcomes the increasing number of new jobs created.
- Empowerment of women was confirmed by their involvement in business activities and social interactions with other group members and BWAs. They now actively participate in household matters

in terms of financial contribution and decision-making process in the family;

- Project has provided benefits to families, particularly women, through the provision of improved access to the banks, property and business education;
- The BWA has enough training and technical capacity and staff to continue and replicate this project to another rayons in the country;
- The RETA of this nature provides an opportunity to finance small NGOs such as BWAs at low cost, requiring minimal processing and ADB resources. It also assists local institutions to develop their GAD capacity, and pilot-test new initiatives.

8

NGOs in Bangladesh

GENDER AND SOCIAL JUSTICE, AIN O SHALISH KENDRO - ASK

Background

As in many countries in the world, legal procedure in Bangladesh is slow and expensive. For most people, the legal system is out of their reach. To avoid costly and lengthy court, people seek local remedies such as the traditional alternative dispute resolution mechanism, popularly known as shalish. Issues such as marital dispute, desertion, oral divorce, maintenance, land and criminal offenses such as rape, adultery, dowry related violence, are commonly dealt with in shalish sessions in Bangladesh.

These sessions tend to be conducted by local government representatives, particularly the Union Chairperson and social leaders such as religious leaders and teachers. For judgment, many of these sessions rely on customary practices and Islamic Shariah laws, often issuing verdicts that not only discriminate against women but also contradict existing legal rights.

To try and correct such discriminatory and illegal verdicts, the national NGO Ain O Shalish Kendro is conducting a Gender and Social Justice program that has its main objective the reform of traditional shalish interpretations and the attitude of shalishkers or mediators. A major strategy here is to develop community awareness and draw on community participation, particularly of women, to persuade local representatives and community leaders to base their shalish decisions on existing laws.

With this in mind, ASK approached ADB for funding to expand its activities into the area of shalish and legal awareness within shalish practices at the local (Union and Ward) level. This builds on ASK's long association with legal rights and legal aid. Established in 1986 by a small group of lawyers, social scientists and development workers, ASK has been providing support to women in the areas of legal counseling, mediation and litigation through its legal aid, advocacy and research activities.

Components

The overall objective of the Gender and Social Justice program is to reduce unlawful shalish judgments and to correct discrimination against women inherent in many shalish practices. The main mechanism to achieve this is the development of Ain Shohayota Committees (ASCs). The role of these ASCs is to monitor arbitration practices as well as to provide a source of arbitration at the Ward level. To achieve this, ASK undertakes a number of community consultations and training programs.

The aim here is to establish strong, socially aware ASCs with sufficient training on legal matters, women's rights and shalish processes to enable them to effect changes in the attitudes and judgments of arbitrators. In terms of the current project, ASCs will be established in six Unions (covering 54 Wards). ASK operates the program in five districts with the support of four donors of which ADB is one. The areas of operation is not specified by donor, so all donors together support the program in the five districts.

- Make local elected representatives and law enforcement agencies sensitive to the principles of gender justice and equality as guaranteed in the Constitution.
- Enable poor women to participate in shalish and other decision making processes to equality of justice.
- Strengthen the capacity of local groups to monitor enforcement mechanisms and advocate alternatives within a democratic system.
- Monitor local shalish by ASC to ensure that it is participatory and gender and socially just.
- Prevent fatwa and unlawful shalish.
- Develop human rights activists at the community level.
- To develop the capacity of partner NGOs to conduct and sustain the program.

To achieve these goals, ASK works in collaboration with sympathetic partner NGOs in the local area. ASK provides its PNGOs with training and legal support. Staff of PNGOs and ASK meet twice yearly in each working area to discuss, review and analyze issues related to implementation. The PNGOs are responsible for implementing as well as monitoring the program.

They therefore select the community organizers who are to mobilize community support for the development of ASCs and ensure their sustainability. The role of the community organizer includes:

- Attending all ASC-related meetings and workshops.
- Developing a good relationship with members of elected bodies.
- Advising on more difficult/complex cases, or referring such cases to the PNOG or ASK for legal aid.

- Monitoring the progress of cases referred to legal aid for court action, including those that cannot be dealt with by shalish (such as rape and murder).
- Providing support to victims, e.g. by accompanying them to other districts to pursue their case.
- rranging follow-up training for ASC members.

The focal point of the project is the development of effective ASCs. These committees consist of five members, including at least two women. The ASCs operate at the ward-level, with a total of 45 ASC members in each Union (there are nine wards per union). They are recruited during Union-level workshops organized by ASK. While this process is conducted with the cooperation of the local elected bodies, ASC members are not themselves local elected representatives. It is important that the ASCs maintain an independence so that they can be seen as an impartial monitoring and consultation unit.

Following selection, ASC members receive training and participate in workshops designed by ASK to develop their legal awareness and mediation skills. Recruits receive an initial 3-day training, where they are provided with easy to read materials on how to mediate disputes, training in common legal issues, and strategies on how to prevent unlawful shalish. Common legal topics covered in the training include legal rights of children, bride price, dower, shalish, marriage registration, divorce, Muslim and Christian Family Law, Muslim inheritance law, Family Law Ordinance (1988), guardianship, etc.

To support the activities and training needs of ASC member, there are on going monthly review meetings. Generally, three ASCs meet every month (with a total of 15 members). There is also a monthly meeting of all ASCs in one union. The community organizer and ASK's lawyers also attend all meetings in order to provide advice and refer complicated cases to ASK, partner NGOs, such as MUKTI and to the police and court as needed.

ASC activities are also supported by popular theater teams, which complement the project but are not directly funded by it. Popular theater draws on the talent and enthusiasm of local actors and musicians to raise awareness about women's legal rights and legal provisions related to common problems such as dowry, divorce, polygamy, violence against women, etc. Performances are informal making use of limited props and resources, and generally reflect on a recent issue in the area. Following the performance, the audience is asked to comment on and discuss the issue raised. Popular theater teams usually comprise about 15 members and are established at the union level. Popular theater teams also receive some training, similar to that provided to ASC members.

According to three ASC members interviewed in the district of Kushtia, the work of ASC members is similar to that of community workers. Although unpaid, they give their time in order to help the predominantly poor residents in their ward settle conflict through arbitration. The two farmers and house wife interviewed agreed that ASC activities were having an influence on local affairs. They already claim to have had some success in mediating disputes (see Sultana's Story below), as little-by-little, more people bring their troubles to ASC members. They have also been able to work with the police to lay charges against a few offenders under the new Women's and Children's Repression Act (2000). Consequently, they report a decline in the extent of violence against women in the area.

The female ASC member said how women's participation as ASC members was particularly important given that the main issues and conflicts they deal with relate to family matters and violence against women. She said that many women would not confide such personal matters to men and prefer to deal with female ASC members. These ASC members also worked closely with the Popular Theater Team, which at times worked to garner public support for victims involved in unsettled disputes.

Sultana's Story

After the sudden death of her husband from lightning, Sultana found life with her husband's family increasingly unbearable due to the constant verbal and physical abuse she received from her mother-in-law. In the end, she fled to her parents' house shortly after the birth of her son. However, her husband's family would not allow her to take her baby with her, so once back with her parents, she approached ASC for help.

Because her in-laws lived in another district, ASC members - together with the ASK community organizer - approached ASC members and the police in that district. Through a process of arbitration, involving ASC members from both districts, the young widow was eventually reunited with her baby in her parents' home.

TWO PLAYS BY THE POPULAR THEATER TEAM

Domestic Dispute

This story was based on a case that ASC was involved with but unable to solve. A young woman was abandoned by her husband in her parents' home following a domestic dispute. The case came to ASC as the young woman wanted to resume living with her husband, but his parents were against it. ASC tried to facilitate a reunion but failed; the case was then referred to MUKTI, but to no avail. Finally, the Popular Theatre Team developed a drama based on the story of an unhappy, abandoned wife. This lead to a happy ending with the young woman once again living with her husband.

A Warning Against Early Marriage

This play was developed by the Popular Theater Team to discourage early marriage for young women and girls. In developing the play, the Team consulted with the marriage registrar and used materials provided by ASK. They also drew on local experiences to highlight the negative consequences for women of early marriage, including their withdrawal from school, the effect on young women's psychological development and early pregnancy. The play was quite controversial and resulted in a lot of discussion, with the performers believing that the play has made a difference to local attitudes.

FUTURE DIRECTIONS

There is potential to replicate elements of this project in wards and unions throughout Bangladesh. Working with other partner NGOs, ASK has the legal experience and institutional capacity to manage such a project.

ADB could also build on this project to consider the role of shalish and the potential of ASC as alternative dispute resolution (ADR) mechanisms in ADB-financed legal and judicial reforms. In particular, ADB should build on the training modules and experience learned during this project to promote legal and shalish reforms that respect the rights of women, work within the existing laws of Bangladesh and monitor the incidence of illegal shalish rulings and procedures.

There is also scope to consider shalish and ADR in future program loans and technical assistance targeting violence against women. The very personal nature of such crimes often inhibits women from approaching formal police avenues. The cost of pursuing police and court action is of course another barrier here. The Ministry of Women and Children Affairs and the Ministry of Law and Parliamentary

Affairs could act as executing agencies for Government projects in this area.

ENHANCING INSTITUTIONAL CAPACITY OF FEMALE-HEADED MICRO FINANCE NGOS - CREDIT AND DEVELOPMENT FORUM

Background

NGOs in Bangladesh such as the Grameen Bank and BRAC have gained international recognition for their innovative approaches to microfinance for employment and income generation, especially for women. What is perhaps less well known is the large number of smaller female-headed NGOs providing microfinance to women throughout Bangladesh.

These organizations provide an invaluable service by targeting women not served by the larger microfinance organizations. They also account for a higher proportion of women in microfinance organizations in leadership positions. While about 85 percent of members of microfinance programs are women, women occupy only about 10 percent of leadership positions. This highly skewed leadership pattern is most acute in the larger microfinance programs, in contrast to the smaller female-headed microfinance NGOs.

The small-scale and locally-based nature of these female-headed NGOs brings both opportunities and constraints. While enabling them to access very poor women in more isolated districts, their size and experience poses problems for their development as an organization.

In particular, small women's NGOs lack skills in the areas of staff and financial management. With only a small number of staff - all heavily involved in the operations and service-delivery side - it is very difficult for such NGOs to develop their skills and institutional capacity or access training.

The Credit and Development Forum (CDF), an umbrella NGO representing microfinance NGOs in Bangladesh, is well aware of such constraints. Representing more than 900 microfinance organizations - including 81 female-headed NGOs - CDF is committed to meeting the training and organizational development needs of its partner NGOs. Recognizing that most of its female-headed partner NGOs faced particular hurdles in terms of capacity building and training, CDF approached ADB for financial support to develop and deliver specific training modules to strengthen the institutional capacity of these female-headed NGOs. A long term goal of the project is to build the institutional capacity of these female-headed NGOs in order that they can qualify for Palli Karma Sahayak Foundation (PKSF) funding. Access to such funds would greatly expand the range of projects and financial resources available to these female-headed microfinance NGOs.

Components

The primary objective of the project is to strengthen the institutional capacity of female-headed microfinance NGOs so that they can expand their outreach, track their program performance, maintain accounts and related records, tap necessary resources, and provide dynamic leadership in order to provide quality financial services to women clients. The project seeks to provide one year extended support for capacity building in management, financial information systems and supervision and monitoring. Two staff from each NGO will be trained. The project is broken down into two stages, that is, the selection of project partners and the capacity development phase.

Out of the total 81 female-headed NGOs, 20 agreed to take part in the project. Participating organization have agreed to cover their own transportation costs, but will receive training materials and live-in accommodation during the training programs at no cost. To qualify, these female-headed NGOs had to meet the following criteria:

- A minimum of 500 active members
- A minimum of TK 1 million loans transacted
- Interested, but as yet unable, to qualify for PKSF funding.

The capacity development phase includes the following components:

- Five-day training course on supervision and monitoring savings and credit management.
- Five-day training course on microfinance related accounts management.
- Five-day training course on management information systems.
- CDF is also considering organizing follow up training and reviews at the end of the project at its own expense.

Several participants noted that even the selection process was an exercise in training. They found great difficulty in providing the range of information required by CDF as part of a base-line survey of the selected project participants. This reinforced to them the need for more systematic record keeping and financial information systems.

Outcomes

The project is still in its first year of operation. Ultimately, the project hopes to deliver the following outcomes:

- Baseline surveys on the profiles of 30-35 small and medium-sized female-headed NGOs.
- Strengthen leadership ability of CEOs in the participating NGOs.

- Improve efficiency levels in the participating female-headed NGOs.
- Provide a model for capacity-building of female-headed NGOs which may be replicated in other projects.

The project is still in an early stage of implementation. To date, project beneficiaries have attended several meetings and workshops, and one training course has been organized on microfinance-related accounts management. Nevertheless, comments from a number of project participants reveal their enthusiasm for and appreciation of the project so far:

"I belong to a small organization committed to improving the status of women. While we have established a small fund for microcredit, we feel that we lack organizational skills in areas such as management and financial systems. We need to be better organized and make our financial information and record-keeping more systematic. We tend to take advantage of the training when it is available as we have limited resources."

"Apart from technical skills, women-headed organizations have specific issues. So one of the attractions of this project is that it provides a forum for women to share experiences, problems and solutions."

"Our organization works in more isolated areas, and being part of this project has been very informative. We didn't know that women were working at various levels. The workshops have exposed us to new ideas on how to develop our organization. Preparing accounting information for CDF has already helped us. In the last meeting, CDF said that it will help us access [qualify for] PKSF funds."

"We need resources in terms of technical skills to reach the poorest-of-the-poor. No other forum has done this, treat women-headed micro-credit organizations as a separate group of stakeholders."

One female CEO gave her own story as an example of what can be achieved. She said that seven years ago she lived in full purdah but that as a result of her work in microfinance she has gained the confidence to actively participate in society and to deal with men. She has also developed strategies to maintain good relations with local hooligans, such as inviting them to share a cup of tea with her and explaining to them the nature of her organization.

The importance of maintaining good relations with the community was a point made by all the women, who were particularly aware of the risks facing female credit staff who disburse and collect money. Many of the women present expressed concern over the presence of gangs and hooligans in rural areas. While male credit staff share the dangers here, sexual violence was an additional risk faced primarily by female credit staff.

Although not considered in the original project proposal, CDF is developing additional training for these women in the area of gender and development. Because this training was not included in CDF's original project proposal, CDF will fund this component themselves or seek donor support. The decision to provide additional training in the areas of gender and development is in response to the needs of the project beneficiaries, who despite having acquired a wealth of practical and experiential knowledge on women's role and status in their communities, have an uneven understanding of concepts such as gender, empowerment, and gender and development.

During this meeting, several participants expressed interest in learning more about other female-headed NGOs working in the area of gender and development and relevant government initiatives and policies. To assist CDF, they are looking to recruit a training manager with experience in the field of microfinance and gender and development. CDF is also considering holding an annual convention for female-headed microfinance NGOs, both partners and non-partners to build up participants' experience and exposure to this important area.

Increasing the gender capacity of CDF via the development of new gender training modules and the recruitment of a gender specialist has also had positive benefits for CDF as an institution.

As a result, CDF is also considering revising its training materials and statistical analyses in order to raise awareness of gender and empowerment as critical issue in microfinance and support gender disaggregated data collection. These changes will in turn help to develop the gender capacity of CDF's partner NGOs - both female-headed and male-headed.

FUTURE DIRECTION

Poverty reduction is the overarching priority of ADB's Country Strategy and Program (CSP) for Bangladesh, with 47 percent of the 17 projects in the 2002-2004 lending program poverty intervention projects. Gender is also a thematic priority in the CSP, in line with ADB's own policy on gender and development.

There is scope, therefore, to build on this technical assistance particularly in the areas of poverty reduction and gender equity. For example, many ADB-funded poverty reduction and rural and urban infrastructure projects in Bangladesh include a microfinance component directed at women. ADB therefore should consider inclusion of capacity building activities of female-headed microfinance NGOs in its future support for microfinance projects.

Capacity building of female-headed microfinance NGOs also contributes to women's empowerment and gender mainstreaming. This is in line with ADB's own objectives as well as government directives such as the National Policy for the Advancement of Women.

The ability to increase the number of female-headed NGOs which qualify for PKSF funding will also help redress the highly skewed gender imbalance at leadership levels within microfinance NGOs.

In addition to extending similar training to female-headed microfinance NGOs not included in the current project, additional technical assistance could be provided in order build the institutional capacity of female-headed NGOs in other sectors, such as those working in the areas of adult education and female literacy, and women's health and family planning.

ADB can also play a dialogue role here, particularly in regards to developing special funding mechanisms within the PKSF for female-headed microfinance NGOs. Support for such an initiative could be sought from the National Poverty Reduction Council as well as the Ministry of Women and Children Affairs.

The National Poverty Reduction Council is a policy making body recently formed but not yet active. It may support the development of a gender sensitive credit policy for poverty reduction led by Bangladesh Bank and the Ministry of Women and Children Affairs. As ADB is considering technical assistance to the National Poverty Reduction Council, specifically to develop the capacity of its Poverty Monitoring Cell, ADB could also consider technical assistance to strengthen the gender analysis and gender-sensitive monitoring capacity of the National Poverty Reduction Council and Poverty Monitoring Cell.

The Poverty Monitoring Cell could then investigate the feasibility and evaluate the role of special funding mechanisms for female-headed NGOs as a poverty reduction strategy.

WATER BLUES TELEFILM ON ARSENIC POISONING IN BANGLADESH — FEMCOM

Background: Arsenic poisoning is a growing problem in Bangladesh. Arsenocosis is caused by drinking arsenic-tainted groundwater, a major problem in the country due to high levels of bacterial pollution in surface water. The disease causes many problems including vomiting and diarrhea; abdominal pain; muscular pain; skin rashes; and swelling of the eyelids, feet and hands. Arsenocosis ultimately affects the heart, lungs, and kidneys and can be fatal. The World Health Organization has described the naturally occurring arsenic as the largest mass poisoning of a population in history. It warns that up to 80 million Bangladeshis may be affected. While various nongovernment organizations (NGOs) involved in water and sanitation activities are working with the Department of Public Health and Engineering to eradicate arsenic from water supplies, it is necessary to educate the population about the dangers of using arsenic-tainted water, the treatments available, and actions they can take to avoid Arsenocosis.

Recognizing the need for an accessible and widely disseminated education campaign, the NGO FemCom researched and developed the film Patal Purir Galpo. The title translates as Story from Under the Earth though the English version was titled Water Blues. The film was conceived as a preventive health initiative to convey information about arsenic poisoning to a broad audience using a popular cultural medium and well-known actors and performers.

Pre-production

A screenplay was developed after consultation with victims of arsenic poisoning, health officials, and the arsenic programs of various NGOs. Popular television and theater performers were contacted and the press was invited to a discussion of the issues. Feedback from this session was then incorporated into the screenplay. It was also decided to incorporate songs composed and performed by well-known musicians into the film to enhance its appeal to a wide audience.

Production

The telefilm was shot in Gazipur, Ashulia, Singair and in villages with arsenic-tainted water supplies. Local residents were recruited to assist in various activities including the identification of Arsenocosis patients. FemCom was pleased to find that the patients were happy to participate and took their enthusiasm as an indication of their level of faith in the project, that is, the patients' belief that the film would succeed in informing the government and fellow citizens and in finding solutions to their problems. The involvement of popular film and television personalities was seen as a great coup in this respect. Not only did they build a strong rapport with arsenic patients, they also guaranteed a wide audience for the film. Other inputs came from various NGOs and from villagers and health care workers who educated the performers and advised on script and set details.

Post-Production

The film was edited and reviewed by various arsenic experts and by villagers of Manikganj. The villagers were positive in their responses to the film and found it informative and enjoyable to watch. The Bangladesh Television Authority agreed to broadcast the telefilm on their national media channel, and it was edited into a final copy. An English subtitled version was produced to enable screening to other South Asian countries that also experience problems with arsenic-tainted water. This version was also useful for screenings with non-Bangladeshi dignitaries and for workshops, conferences, and seminars attended by non-Bangladeshi audiences.

Publicity and Presentation

The premier was attended by many dignitaries, representatives of various organizations, the production team, and cast members. Publicity for the film highlighted the involvement of popular performers and emphasized the film as an entertaining portrayal of an important issue. The film was deemed a great success and was recognized as portraying an important message in an engaging form. The screening was covered by all the daily newspapers and film magazines and was acclaimed as a significant contribution to raising awareness about arsenic poisoning in Bangladesh. Viewer's reports in the newspapers were also positive. The screening on Bangladesh TV was also received warmly by viewers, and the film was rated in the TV guide as the best telefilm of the year.

Interest has also been expressed in screening the film on a number of nongovernment channels such as ETV, Channel 1 and ATN Bangla. It has also been screened in India. FemCom would like to produce a 35mm version for screening in cinemas to enable the film to reach audiences that do not have access to television. The project has been enormously successful in achieving its goals of informing a wide audience about an important issue through a popular form of entertainment. The enthusiastic response by audiences, the media, and television stations shows the potential of this medium, if thoughtfully utilized, for achieving important social outcomes.

COMBATING VIOLENCE AGAINST WOMEN AND CHILDREN-MUKTI NARI O SHISHU KALYAN SHANGSTHA

Background: The number of violent acts against women – including acid throwing, rape, trafficking and other sexual violence – are of great concern to women's NGOs and other organizations in Bangladesh. The frequency of such violence is evidence that the formal structures of law and policing fail to protect women and children. Poverty, low literacy and lack of awareness of legal rights work against women seeking redress through formal mechanisms. For poor women, the court system is financially beyond their reach and the police viewed with suspicion. Women's capacity to utilize the courts and police is further limited by the male-dominated structures and discriminatory practices embedded in these institutions. What is urgently required in such cases are mediating organizations operating at the local level which can intervene on the victim's behalf to demand legal and police support, as well as pursue – where more appropriate – alternative dispute resolution mechanism.

Donor organizations, however, do not have the organizational capacity to pursue such grassroots activities. They are better placed to influence governments in the areas of legal reform and gender sensitization. While such reforms are critical, they do not necessarily help poor women who are victims of violence.

For women burdened with low levels of literacy and no independent financial resources there are overwhelming practical barriers to applying to the court for justice. Recognizing this situation, ADB took the initiative of working directly with a local level NGO in order to foster new mechanisms for supporting the needs of poor women who are victims of violence. In doing so, ADB also recognized that local-level NGOs can also make a contribution to the areas of legal and judicial reform. In particular, the knowledge that such organizations develop in dealing with the practical, structural and cultural barriers faced by poor women when accessing the legal and police systems can in turn feed into government reform strategies.

The NGO in question is MUKTI Nari-O-Shishu Kalyan Shangstha, operating in the Kushtia district of western Bangladesh. With a female lawyer as Executive Director, the strength of this organization is its capacity to utilize formal legal and police structures as well as traditional arbitration practices (shalish).

Since its inception in 1990, MUKTI has provided legal aid to female victims of violence and injustice, particularly in those areas that most affect women, that is, sexual violence, divorce, dowry, early marriage and polygamy. It has also monitored cases referred to various union-level Shalish Committees across six thanas in the Kushtia district. MUKTI has experienced first hand the increase in violence against women as a result of increasing dowry expectations and the trafficking in women over this time. (Kushtia as a border district is often used as a route for trafficking of women and girls) It is also a very poor area, and very few women victims have access to or get support from the police or courts.

Components

With support from RETA 5889, MUKTI undertook a number of activities designed to sensitize various stakeholders on the problem of violence against women. As a result of these workshops, a process of dialogue developed between MUKTI and local stakeholders, including the police, the media, lawyers, government, etc. Funds were also spent on strengthening MUKTI's research capacity through the development of a database on the incidence and handling of VAW cases in local hospitals and police stations.

Major project components were:

- Observation and monitoring of government organizations (courts, hospitals, police stations, etc.) related to violence against women

- Gender-sensitization and other training and orientation of key stakeholders, including representatives of women's organizations, journalists, government, lawyers, police personnel, etc.
- Establish processes for advocacy and lobbying
- Research, publication and information dissemination

Outcomes

Over the course of the project, a total of 24 workshops will be run to raise awareness on violence against women and to build a platform for advocacy and lobbying. In particular, the workshop-cum-dialogue sessions will strengthen MUKTI's relationships with the courts, the police and other local government organizations.

To date, workshops held at the district and thana-levels have enabled MUKTI to establish high-level dialogue with the Police Superintendent, Civil Surgeon, the District Women's Affairs Officer, the District Coordinator of Non-Formal Education, the Assistant Director of Horticulture in the Department of Agriculture, social workers, journalists, lawyers and others. MUKTI has received a letter of support from the Civil Surgeon and the Police Superintendent allowing MUKTI to observe cases of violence against women in hospitals and police stations. MUKTI is also a member of the district-level government Committee on Violence Protection. This type of involvement at the district level will ensure the sustainability of the project and of MUKTI into the future.

Other positive outcomes from the project include the establishment of a database on crimes against women, including violent crimes. The collection and classification of such data has benefited from the involvement of ADB's GAD specialist. Such information feeds back into raising local awareness as disseminated in the media and via

MUKTI's own training programs. For this reason, MUKTI arranges press conferences and includes journalists in the project's workshops. This research component also provides important policy-related data on the incidence and reporting of VAW in the Kushtia area.

Case Study 1. Rupa

Rupa was a young woman of 16 when sold into trafficking by her husband. Tragically, the story is not unique in Bangladesh. A woman from a poor family, she married a man from outside her district. Her husband approached her family asking to marry Rupa, and they agreed. For young women of Rupa's background, marriage and motherhood are the only acceptable social roles. For young women from poor families, there is an additional obligation to marry so as not to be a financial burden on their family.

Unfortunately Rupa's new husband was linked to a gang involved in trafficking young women to supply brothels in Dhaka. Very shortly after their marriage, he took Rupa to Dhaka and had her held in a house until he could arranged for her sale. In the meantime, her husband informed Rupa's parents that their daughter was missing. This made them immediately suspicious but they did not know what to do. Rupa's mother said that they did not go to the police with their problem as they thought the police would ask for money to pursue the matter, and they had none. Desperate but without any hope, they heard about MUKTI from people in the local area. MUKTI immediately set about recovering their daughter. Representatives from MUKTI went to the district police, who then advised police in other areas, including Dhaka. Fortunately for Rupa, she managed to escape from the house in which she was being held. Police found her in Dhaka and placed her in protective custody. Lawyers from MUKTI arranged for her release and she was brought back to her parent's house, where she now lives.

According to Rupa's mother, Rupa's recovery would not have been possible without MUKTI's assistance. In particular, MUKTI's good relationship with the district police and judiciary meant that the police responded to this case with speed. The police later arrested Rupa's brother-in-law but her husband absconded and Rupa's parents did not have the resources to press charges or pursue the matter further. In the end, through intermediaries, they settled on a divorce. We need resources in terms of technical skills to reach the poorest-of-the-poor. No other forum has done this, treat women-headed micro-credit organizations as a separate group of stakeholders.

MUKTI's assistance did not end there. MUKTI's intervention also made possible Rupa's acceptance back into local society. In conservative rural Bangladesh, a woman's honor is important to her status as well as her family's status. While divorce is tolerated, women risk social ostracism if associated with prostitution and other illicit sexual relations. When Rupa first returned from Dhaka there were numerous rumors suggesting that Rupa had in fact been working as a prostitute during the time she was held in protective custody. The lack of a court case or charges seemed to falsify Rupa's version of events. To facilitate Rupa's acceptance by the local community, MUKTI arranged for Rupa to make a signed statement in front of a magistrate. The police in Dhaka then verified that she was in police custody during the time in question. Following this, MUKTI held several meetings with influential local groups, where Rupa's story was explained and her statement shown as evidence. Currently, Rupa is living with her family and training to be a tailor as part of the Department of Women's Affairs skills development program for women's self-reliance.

Case Study 2. Asma and Jamil

Marriage in Bangladesh is rarely a decision taken by two individuals. In general, families make marriages. So when senior family members disapprove of a marriage - such as the husband's mother or father - the family will often take steps to break up a marriage. This is what happened in the case of Asma and Jamil's marriage. Asma and Jamil had been married for ten years. They have a seven year old daughter. Jamil's mother, however, was never happy about the match. Firstly, Asma came from a poor family and did not bring much in the way of dowry. Secondly, Asma does not have the use of her legs and so cannot work in the house or field like other wives. For many years, Asma and Jamil lived separately from Jamil's family, as the family would not accept Asma. Finally, Jamil was told that he would not inherit any property unless he divorced his wife. Under pressure from his family and to get some money from them, he moved back home, where he stayed for four months. During this time, he was almost held in custody by his family and refused all contact with this wife. His family relentlessly pressured him to remarry, which he eventually did. However, Jamil refused to consummate the marriage out of respect for Asma. When Asma went to visit Jamil at his family's home, she was beaten by his brother and brother's wife. Asma reported this to the police, who were reluctant to get involved in what they saw as a domestic dispute. Someone in the police station suggested she try MUKTI.

In such situations, MUKTI appeals to the traditional arbitration mechanism, shalish. At the NGO's headquarters, MUKTI brings together all the parties involved, as well as a few socially respected elders or local leaders. Shalish is essentially a process of dialogue which allows the issues to be aired frankly and seeks to reach a settlement on the basis of socially accepted values and norms. Shalish relies on social norms and the very public nature of any agreements or settlements to change people's behavior and ensure they live up to the commitments made during shalish. Usually an agreement is only reached over the course of several meeting. Once an agreement is reached, it is put in writing and the parties asked to sign it. In some cases, those involved are asked to report to MUKTI on a regular basis to monitor the situation. In this case, widely accepted norms supporting marriage, particularly when there is a child involved, where brought into play to pressure Jamil's family to accept his marriage to Asma. As a result of the shalish process initiated by MUKTI, Asma and Jamil are now living together again and his family has agreed not to disinherit him. His second wife continues to live with her parents, as the father-in-law of Jamil is demanding money for a divorce. MUKTI is also dealing with this issue in order to free Asma from the status of co-wife. As in other such cases, the direct involvement of MUKTI's executive director, a respected lawyer was central in reaching a solution acceptable to all parties.

Future Direction

MUKTI's database and dialogue process with district government organizations has the potential to feed into other government initiatives, including policy making and efforts to prevent violence against women as discussed in the Bangladesh National Policy for the Advancement of Women. MUKTI has already begun to build on the relationships formed through this project. For example, recognizing the relationship between literacy, awareness and VAW, MUKTI has plans to work with the Department of Non-Formal Education to deliver adult literacy programs, which will also contain information on women's legal rights, child marriage, and violence against women.

There is potential to scale-up and replicate elements of this project. For example, similar research and dialogue-cum-training workshops could be implemented in other parts of the country, drawing on both MUKTI's approach as well as its links to other Dhaka-based national NGOs such as Ain O Shalish Kendro (ASK) and Naripokkho (who assisted MUKTI with monitoring cases of violence against women brought to hospital).

There is potential for ADB to consider the role of alternative dispute resolution (ADR) in potential legal and judicial reform projects financed by ADB. For example, MUKTI has demonstrated not only the practical value and cost effective nature of alternative dispute resolution but the ways in which ADR can work within and support other legal and police structures. The strengthening of arbitration processes such as Shalish Committees is also part of such a reform agenda. This would compliment another project supported under RETA 5889 by the national NGO, Ain O Shalish Kendro (ASK). There is also scope to consider VAW and ADR in future program loans, drawing on support of the Ministry of Women and Children's Affairs, the National Policy for the Advancement of Women and the Ministry of Law and Parliamentary Affairs. A first step is to build on issues of deteriorating law and order and violence against women as discussed in ADB's Country Assistance Plan Strategy 2000-2003 for Bangladesh. VAW and ADR should be included as components of other sectoral loans (e.g. in health, rural and urban development, poverty reduction projects, etc.), as well as addressed in project loans primarily related to the development of efficient and responsive legal and administrative frameworks in Bangladesh. Technical assistance projects could also be funded in the areas of VAW and ADR.

WOMEN WITH DISABILITIES - CAMBODIAN DISABLED PEOPLE'S ORGANISATION

Objectives

The overall objective of the project was to address the needs of women living with disabilities by developing networks of support for them and assisting them to benefit from available technical and training resources. It was also anticipated that the priorities, roles, and participation of women with disabilities in both community activities and in the Cambodian Disabled People's Organisation (CDPO) would be strengthened as a result.

The specific objectives of the project were the following:

- to develop networks of women with disabilities to protect, serve, and promote their rights, achievements, and interests in order to bring about their fuller participation and equality in society
- to further the rights and interests of women with disabilities by establishing or strengthening self-help groups in which they can raise and address relevant social and economic issues
- to strengthen the voices of women with disabilities, raise public awareness about their interests and concerns, and identify their skills in order to address their needs

To develop networks, the CDPO's Active Women's Group conducted monthly meetings with representatives of national and international organizations, including the national nongovernment organization (NGO) Forum, and four to six weekly meetings with the Disability Action Council. Two workshops and a number of training programs for CPDO staff and members facilitated the development of self-help groups and of self-awareness of shared issues. A workshop titled "Women with Disabilities Awareness" was organized in conjunction with the Disability Action Council and drew 24 participants representing a number of affiliated organizations and ministries including a number of organizations in rural areas. Feedback on this workshop showed that participants enjoyed the opportunity to share information and deepen their understanding of issues contributing to the lack of self-confidence and poor living standards of disabled women. A two-day training workshop on disability and society was organized by CDPO for 25 invited participants including a number of representatives of rural organizations. As a result of this workshop, participants

- shared information about their situations
- analyzed some of the factors behind discrimination against disabled people
- gained confidence to establish self-help groups in the provinces

Finally, the project team recognized the need to raise both the voices of women with disabilities and public awareness in order to dispel myths and stereotypes. A public awareness campaign was conducted over the 6 months of the project which included radio interviews with disabled women and articles in newspapers and journals.

Outcomes

This project resulted in a number of positive outcomes for both women with disabilities and for CDPO. Through meetings with the Women's Active Group, disabled women have gained self-confidence in solving the problems they face. There are also now more avenues for disabled women and girls to pursue work and education following training and information sessions with parents and community groups. For example, following discussions with staff from the Women's Active Group, more families are willing to allow their disabled daughters to take up work and school opportunities outside the home. The Women's Active Group has also been recognized by the Ministry of Women's and Veterans' Affairs and has been invited to participate in relevant seminars, such as those on gender and development, and major events including the 2001 International Women's Day march in which 120 women with disabilities participated. Further evidence of strengthened advocacy can be seen in the following examples.

The Ministry of Education has begun to understand the need for disability awareness and to accept children with disabilities in schools. The Women's Active Group was asked to contribute to the Convention to End all Forms of Discrimination Against Women's report on the Beijing+5 Meeting where it was noted that the needs of women with disabilities had been overlooked. Their concerns were subsequently included. The Women's Active Group participated in a 16-day Committee on Domestic Violence, and one member of the group was invited to attend the follow-up workshop in Phnom Penh The general public's understanding of issues related to women with disabilities has also been enhanced by radio programs and other awareness-raising activities conducted during the project. For example, the Women's Media Centre of Cambodia used stories of women with disabilities prepared by CDPO in their bulletin and radio program on station FM 102, and two disabled women were interviewed about the issues they faced on station FM 103.

CDPO has also strengthened its organizational capacity and understanding of relevant issues of disabled women. Also, significant skills have been developed within the Women's Active Group. The core staff has learned how to establish self-help groups as a means for providing social and economic support to women with disabilities. They have gained specific skills such as managing, planning, and facilitating projects and organizing workshops. One staff member attended the International Accessibility Campaign in Bangkok that attracted over 600 delegates from Asia and the Pacific. This gave her the opportunity to meet women from different countries and share strategies on how to achieve recognition from their respective governments and greater public awareness of the issues confronting disabled women.

9

NGOs Working for Women in India

STRENGTHENING GOVERNMENT-CITIZEN CONNECTIONS IN URBAN LOCAL BODIES — CENTER FOR SOCIAL RESEARCH

Background: The rate of urbanization has increased rapidly in India over recent years. The distribution of the population shows that this growth has concentrated in larger cities and towns at the expense of smaller towns. This puts enormous pressure on the resources of large municipalities; most are unable to keep up with the provision of even basic services and infrastructure. The irregular availability of basic services like water, sanitation, and public amenities (such as streetlights, parking lots, bus stops, and public conveniences) has aggravated risks to public health and safety. The uneven concentration of the population is partly due to urban policies that encourage the concentration of development in some regions. In other words, urban and regional planning has sometimes exacerbated the problems of larger towns and cities.

Good governance involves more than the direct provision of goods and services. According to the Global Plan of Action adopted during the Second United Nations Conference on Human Settlement (Habitat II), governance is also an approach that enhances the achievement of sustainable human settlements. It involves three main strategies:

- decentralizing responsibilities and resources to local authorities
- encouraging the participation of civil society; and (iii) using partnerships to achieve common objectives

It is in this context that the Government of India introduced the 74th Constitutional Amendment Act (CAA) that gave recognition and impetus to municipalities as democratic units of self-governance. It was expected that decentralization initiated by the act would promote interaction between councilors and the people and would produce local governments that could address the needs of specific municipalities. It recognized that decentralizing without devolving administrative and financial power can result in the failure of local government. A particular feature of the act was the reservation of one-third of seats for women at all levels of urban local bodies (ULB) to address the deficiency of women's representation in government.

The Center for Social Research has conducted several local, national, and regional studies on gender, democracy, and governance. The current study aims to assess the efficacy of the local governments in two large cities in relation to the provisions of the 74th CAA. It aims to promote effective governance by enhancing the capacity of various stakeholders including elected councilors, nongovernment organizations (NGOs), corporate houses, local associations, people's groups, and women and by strengthening links between stakeholders to increase accountability and transparency in the system.

Components

The governance study was carried out in two districts of Rajasthan: Jaipur and Jodphur. Rajasthan has experienced a rapid increase in urbanization due the influx of people from rural areas. Migrants are drawn to the larger towns and cities as they look for more permanent, labor-intensive, nonagricultural employment.

Rajasthan, Jaipur, and Jodphur were selected for a number of reasons. Firstly, Rajasthan has gone through two ULB elections since the introduction of the 74th CAA. This provided an opportunity to analyze the performance of elected members and the effectiveness of the ULBs under the new conditions.

There had also been no major interventions in terms of research or training in regard to governance in Rajasthan's municipal corporations. Jaipur was chosen because it is both the capital of Rajasthan and a popular tourist destination. It has high urban population growth due to the scarcity of land and other resources in its rural hinterland. For these reasons, the pressure on the city for infrastructure and basic amenities is very great. Jodphur was selected because of its geographical location in the western desert area which is highly vulnerable to drought and hence to agricultural scarcities. Jodphur, like Jaipur, is also a world-famous tourist destination. Hence the demand to keep the city clean and well equipped in terms of basic amenities is great. The project began with action research in the selected districts. The aims were as follow:

- to understand and analyze the administrative structure and function of city municipalities
- to measure the extent of devolution of power and resources to the ULBs
- to determine the socioeconomic profile of councilors as well as the barriers they faced, especially women and those economically disadvantaged
- to identify gaps between the desired and the current levels of performance

- to explore the possibility of establishing links with other local stakeholders

Councilors, administrative staff, corporate houses, NGOs, and citizens' groups were identified as key stakeholders in local governance. Interviews and discussion groups were conducted among them using questionnaires tailored to each group. The questionnaires asked respondents about

- their socioeconomic profiles
- electoral backgrounds
- knowledge of legislation, especially the provisions of the 74th CAA

Respondents were also asked to comment on

- the extent of devolution of power in the municipality
- the nature of governance skills
- the impact of gender
- the importance of collaboration for achieving governance goals

The data collected from the fieldwork was supplemented by secondary data collected from published and unpublished sources. It offered a detailed picture of the problems and the knowledge levels of the different categories of stakeholders surveyed. From this picture, two training modules were developed aimed at enhancing the knowledge and skills of participants in local government. One training program was developed for councilors. The second addressed the other groups of stakeholders. At the conclusion of the project, a 2-day workshop was organized with government representatives, corporate houses, and NGOs working towards improving local governance. The workshop was held to report on the outcomes of the research and training, to share strategies aimed at improving the functioning of municipalities, and to analyze the implications of the involvement of different stakeholders.

A research advisory committee was constituted at the head office, and a regional advisory committee was formed locally. These committees advised on the direction, methodology, and implementation of the project.

Outcomes

Devolution of Power

The study revealed that the devolution of power and functions achieved thus far had caused significant problems for municipalities. Many parallel institutions had been created during this process such as the Jaipur Development Authority and Urban Improvement Trust to whom various municipal functions and funds were transferred. This reduced the capacity of the municipalities themselves as they were left with only core functions (sanitation, garbage collection, etc.) and little opportunity for raising revenue. Rather than achieving independence, municipalities then become dependent upon the state government for grants-in-aid or on local taxes for income to discharge their functions.

Women as Emerging Leaders

Women performed well in elections and delivered on their election promises at a higher rate than their male counterparts did. There was a perception among the electorate that female councilors are serious, honest, and committed and that they will revitalize Indian politics. Further, female representatives were perceived as working for development, and their presence in ULBs was reported to have improved the efficiency of the municipalities. It was argued by some respondents that some women councilors acted as proxies for male relatives and gave them their political responsibilities. Overall, however, reserving positions for women was viewed positively; it increased the visibility of women in public life and appears to have had a positive effect on community attitudes toward their work.

The majority of female councilors are in politics for the first time and for this reason would benefit from training and skills in governance procedures. Most juggle their civic responsibilities with family responsibilities. Male councilors tend not to have these competing demands and are generally more experienced politicians. Women also experience some difficulties combining public life with the expectations of their traditional roles. Thus business at night or the need to seek permission from family members to leave the home can make council involvement difficult.

Collaboration

Collaboration was recognized by all stakeholders to be the key to effective governance. However, the meaning and purpose of collaboration differed among the stakeholder groups. Corporate houses viewed collaboration as the provision of financial support. NGOs and citizens' groups saw collaboration as raising awareness and mobilizing to place pressure on existing urban bodies. Councilors were reluctant to collaborate because they wished to retain credit for development initiatives. Owing to the reservations and limitations of the stakeholder groups, collaboration in UBLs was found to be nascent or entirely absent. This situation seriously undermines the effectiveness of urban governance. The need for facilitation to bring groups together and find common ground was noted in the study.

Training

The training modules developed and implemented by CSR addressed areas highlighted in the research findings. A participatory model of training was implemented that included games, group discussion, lectures, presentations, role playing, and group projects. The five objectives addressed in the training were

- to promote understanding and analysis of the structure and function of ULBs and participants' roles in them
- to understand and analyze the importance of team building and mechanisms of conflict resolution
- to understand the importance of effective leadership and different leadership styles
- to understand and analyze the importance of planning and effective participation
- to understand and analyze gender as a social construct

The project achieved its goals in both researching and implementing a course of action to strengthen the effectiveness of local governance. The implementation of training modules addressed the needs identified through the research stage and was well regarded in the evaluation. The study also received significant media attention, thus raising awareness of the issues, particularly on the need for collaboration in UBLs. The study notes that such training should be implemented in more districts to promote greater participation by stakeholders. Other recommendations include advocacy at the state and central level to devolve more power to municipalities, training to orient councilors away from party divisions and towards collaboration, and regular interaction among stakeholders to promote effective communication. Strengthening citizen-government connections requires ongoing research, analysis, and the implementation of actions that address the needs identified.

SHAKTI: WOMEN'S EMPOWERMENT AND SOCIO-ECONOMIC DEVELOPMENT — HUMANA PEOPLE TO PEOPLE

Barjee Devi proudly displays her vermicompost beds to visitors. The glow in her eyes says a lot about the satisfaction and joy she feels for being the owner of something she created with her own hands and initiative. Together with 10 other women in her self-help group, Barjee Devi was given practical training on vermiculture including start-up inputs such as worms and basic tools. All trainees subsequently used vermicompost in their fields. Barjee Devi went one step further: building on the success of vermicompost as a sustainable way to increase yields, she sold 100 kg of vermicompost to a farmer in the vicinity.

Apart from the economic benefits from her participation in the project, one of the major benefits has been the growth in her self-esteem and confidence. Prior to the project, Barjee Devi was a shy young woman. Her day was organized around the needs of her husband's household, working both in the home and on their small landholding. Uneducated and poor, she was initially reluctant to take an active part in the self-help group she joined. Over time, however, her involvement grew and she became more confident and started to participate in weekly discussions and in income generating initiatives. Her interest led the way and motivated other women in the group to pursue training in vermiculture.

The project provided other income generating opportunities as well. Like many women who received goats through this project, Smt. Bimla Harijan and Smt. Meera Bunkar dream of becoming professional goat farmers. Goat rearing and milking have proved to be a lucrative business for them, one that has enabled them to provide better lives and education for their children. By contributing money to their families, their status in the family has also improved. In time they hope their families will involve them in future decisions.

Background: Women play a critical role in agriculture in India; they are centrally involved in the production of crops and have primary responsibility for the care of livestock. Despite their important agricultural roles, women in India have little or no decision-making power with respect to adopting sustainable farming practices and other farm-based income generating activities. This reflects women's general lack of power in rural India where decisions regarding their lives are still largely made by the men in their families. In the Shakti project area, women's status is among the lowest in India. Women are married young and upon marriage move to their husbands' households. Married women are completely dependent on their in-laws and husbands who also control their movements outside the house and their interaction with men.

Women cover their faces as soon as they see a man from outside the family and cannot sit down or participate in discussions when men are present. They own little or no property as the dowries they bring with them at marriage become the property of their husbands' families. Most of them have no formal education. While women make a substantial contribution to family income through their work in the fields and at home, they are seen to have little worth, and problems of high maternal and infant mortality, women's health, and pre- and post-natal care are given little serious attention. In this context, self-help groups have proven to be a very successful mechanism for women's empowerment and socioeconomic development. The groups achieved these outcomes by providing a structure and a forum that allow them to meet regularly in order to discuss their common problems, build their confidence and skill bases, and explore sustainable income generating activities.

Nongovernment organizations (NGOs) such as Humana People to People India play a critical role in the establishment and development of women's self-help groups. As in this project, the involvement of NGOs is important in establishing and building group capacity. In many instances this requires considerable negotiation with village men before they will agree to women's involvement. NGOs also provide training in areas such as gender equity and women's rights, basic education, women's health and wellbeing, income generating activities, and sustainable farming. Finally, NGOs support self-help groups with access to microcredit and other inputs for generating income. Without the mediation of NGOs, banks and other lending institutions are unwilling to provide credit to poor, often illiterate women who do not own land or other resources.

Objectives and Components

The primary objectives of this project were women's empowerment and socioeconomic development in 11 villages in the Jaipur District of Rajashtan. This involved establishing 20 women's self-help groups in order to provide the following:

- access to credit, training, and other inputs necessary to undertake income generating activities including vermiculture and goat raising
- a forum for members to discuss and raise awareness on issues of relevance to women such as health, family planning, and gender equity

The project compromised the following activities:

- preparation of the communities for the project by Humana People to People India
- training and capacity building of 11 animators (i.e., one woman from each village was trained as a health and hygiene educator)
- formation and capacity building of 20 self-help groups
- training and awareness raising on women's reproductive health, family planning, child health, gender equity, and women's and human rights
- training and provision of inputs for income generating projects in goat farming and vermicomposting

Outcomes

As the above case studies demonstrate, the success of the project can be assessed not only on economic grounds but also in terms of women's increased sense of self-reliance and confidence. Twenty self-help groups were established with a total membership of 331 women. The following achievements were the result. Women developed functional savings groups with money deposited in a local bank for withdrawal by the group. The monthly contributions from each member ranged from Rs.10 to Rs.50. depending on the group. Each village received 50 capacity-building and training sessions (550 in total). These sessions covered

- gender and women
- nutrition and women
- violence and women
- work-related hazards and women's health
- reproductive health and family planning
- HIV/AIDS
- training in papaya growing, vermicomposting, and goat rearing

In terms of income generating activities

- 11 women received vermicomposting training and start-up units
- three women received additional training on the use of vermicomposting in growing chilies, wheat and peas
- 47 women received training in goat farming and goats (with most women receiving three goats)

Women's Empowerment and Socioeconomic Development

The type of income generating activities pursued by each group was a decision taken by the self-help group and not dictated by Humana or any other outside agencies. Women discussed these issues at length before deciding on their group's course of action.

Many women were keen to be involved in goat rearing as it was not new to the area and many women understood that goats were more profitable than other milking animals. Goat farming was also attractive as a form of income as it is less dependent on the scarce rainfall in the region, on erratic market conditions, and on the high cost of production farming. Once the decision was made, Humana advised the self-help groups that each group could be provided with six goats but that the group had to decide how to distribute or share them. In most cases, the groups decided that the poorest members of the group should be given three goats each and should be trained in goat milking and rearing.

TRANSPORTATION NEEDS OF SELF-EMPLOYED WOMEN — SEWA BANK

Background

Lack of affordable transportation is an issue facing millions of poor, self-employed women working in the informal sector in India. Walking is the most common form of transport for the majority of these women, particularly for the many mobile female peddlers who spend their days hauling heavy head loads and handcarts.

Because of the relatively high cost of paid private transportation, women are forced to limit their use of tempos (motorized rickshaws a little larger than auto-rickshaws), auto-rickshaws, and pedal rickshaws. In many situations, women cannot avail themselves of more affordable public transport because of their bulky, heavy loads. To date, there has been little research into the transportation needs and options of self-employed women in the informal sector. This is an emerging issue for the Shri Mahila Sewa Sahakari Bank in Ahmedabad which has been addressing the credit and savings needs of over 1,250,000 women clients since 1972. An earlier study commissioned by Sewa Bank (My Daily Odyssey in 1998) recommended that further study be undertaken on the professional and personal transportation needs of Sewa Bank's clients. In light of this recommendation, the Asian Development Bank funded Sewa Bank to undertake a transportation needs assessment of its clients to better understand their transportation concerns and priorities, including the viability of extending credit to clients for the purchase of private vehicles.

Components

The objectives of the study were the following:

- to investigate the professional and personal transportation needs of selected Sewa Bank clients
- to document the constraints faced by poor women in the informal sector due to the lack of appropriate and affordable transportation
- to identify the transportation needs of selected clients not currently met by existing public transportation facilities
- to conduct a first-level market survey on the demand for owning vehicles, and on based this to prepare a basic cost benefit analysis to assess the impact of purchasing a vehicle on the net income levels of clients

Five client groups were selected on the basis of their high mobility and transportation needs: vegetable vendors, used clothes peddlers, head loaders/handcart pullers, rag pickers, and mobile vendors. Mobility is a critical issue for all self-employed women but more so for these groups for whom mobility takes a lot of time, physical effort, and money. The study incorporated structured questionnaires as well as focus discussions with each trade group. In total, there were 105 female respondents in the study comprising 29 vegetable vendors, 24 used clothes peddlers, 25 head loaders/handcart pullers, 13 rag pickers, and 14 mobile vendors.

Outcomes

Overview of the Trade Groups

The vegetable vendors had the highest transportation costs of all averaging 52% of the women's monthly incomes. Most arrive at the local wholesale market early in the morning by shared paid private transport or on public transport. Once they have purchased the vegetables to be sold that day, their choice is either to walk or hire paid private transport on their own. For those who buy vegetables by the sack (between 40-60 kilograms in weight), they also have the expense of paying handcart pullers to carry the vegetables to the available transport.

The used clothes peddlers had the second highest transportation costs averaging 37% of their monthly incomes. Typically, used clothes peddlers start out from their homes with a load of utensils or plastic ware that they exchange for clothes. Given the bulky loads they carry, the use of public transportation is not an option. They walk around in search of clients and over the course of the day gradually replace their loads of utensils or plastic ware with a heavier load of clothes. Their normal pattern is to collect clothes 4 days a week and spend 2 days mending, washing, and ironing them to be ready for sale in the Sunday market. They hire auto-rickshaws or tempos to get there. Additional transportation costs include the purchase of exchangeable goods two to three times a month. On average, the rag pickers in the sample used 33.3% of their monthly incomes on transportation costs. These women leave home early with empty sacks, either walking or taking public transport to their predetermined areas. Once they have collected enough discarded paper, plastic, glass, or metal articles, they walk or take a pedal rickshaw to the godowns where their loads are sorted and sold. The cost of the rickshaw is negotiated according to distance and load. Some women make two such rounds a day: one in the early morning and one in the afternoon. The mobile vendors spent on average 26% of their monthly incomes on transportation. The range of goods sold door-to-door by these women included food products, clothes, cosmetics, and jewelry. Consequently, their transportation needs and costs varied considerably depending on the goods they sold, the distance from their homes to the neighborhoods they targeted, and the incomes they earned. Overall, 64% of the women in this sample either walked or used a combination of walking and paid private transport. While the vegetable vendors spent more of their monthly incomes on transportation costs, the physical drudgery of the mobile vendors was higher. This was especially the case with women who carry toplas (head loads) door-to-door. The head loaders/handcart pullers had the lowest transportation costs of the sample, averaging 11% of their monthly incomes. Most of these women either walk or catch public transport to the wholesale market where they work carrying vegetables and other goods within the market and in the nearby vicinity. For most, the choice is either to carry goods on their heads or to hire handcarts on an hourly basis at a cost of Rs.5. Only a few of these women own handcarts.

The Demand for Owning a Form of Transport among Self-Employed Women

Study findings revealed that transportation is clearly an emerging issue for the credit sector with self-employed women reporting an unmet demand for credit to purchase their own forms of transport. Of the total sample, 69.5% percent reported that they would like to acquire their own facility with 45% stating that they would be prepared to seek credit to do so. (The remaining 55% said that they had more pressing credit needs such as housing and working capital.) In terms of the five trade groups, 100% of the rag pickers, 86% of the mobile vendors, 83% of the used clothes vendors, 66% of the vegetable vendors, and 36% of the head loaders said that they would like their own form of transport. Reasons given included the following:

- a significant reduction in time spent on transportation
- a reduction in transportation costs (see below)
- an increase in productivity
- that existing public transport options were unsuitable
- a reduction in physical work-related strain that would have a positive impact on their health
- a vehicle could be an important secondary source of income for the family

Cost Benefit Analysis and Future Directions

Cost benefit analyses done as part of the study endorsed the feasibility of many of these women acquiring private transportation facilities. The following three examples were provided.

Example : This example demonstrates how one woman's physical burden could be dramatically reduced for a cost of less than Rs.3 per day.

Estimated cost	Rs.2000
Loan required	Rs.2000
Rate of interest	17% p.a.
Term of repayment	36 months
Monthly installment	Rs.71.16
Daily installment	Less than Rs.3

Example : A pedal rickshaw for Kesarben (rag picker)

In this example, Kesarben would not only be able to significantly reduce her transportation costs (and physical burden) by the purchase of a pedal rickshaw, she could also use it to provide a source of income for her unemployed husband.

Estimated cost	Rs.3500
Loan required	Rs.3500
Rate of interest	17% p.a.
Term of repayment	36 months
Monthly installment	Rs.124.53
Vehicle maintenance (per month)	Rs.50
Total monthly transport cost (proposed)	Rs.174.53
Current monthly transport costz	Rs.600

Example : An auto-rickshaw for Abedaben (mobile vendor)

While in this example Abedaben would have to pay more than she currently does on transportation to cover the cost of an auto-rickshaw, she is confident that she would be able to divert the family's other commuting expenses of Rs.2000 per month towards the loan repayment. She also believes that her son would be able to earn more money as a rickshaw driver than he currently earns as a mechanic and hence could also contribute to the loan repayment.

Estimated cost	Rs.70,000
Loan required	Rs.70,000
Rate of interest	17% p.a.
Term of repayment	60 months
Monthly installment	Rs.1733.90
Vehicle fuel and maintenance (per month)	Rs.500
Total monthly transport cost (proposed)	Rs.2233.90
Current monthly transport cost	Rs.1000

BIBLIOGRAPHY

Antti Pentikaiinen: *Creating Global Governance - The Role of Non-Governmental Organizations in the United Nations,* Helsinki, Finnish UN Association 2000.

Aptekar, Lewis. *Street children of Cali,* Durham, Duke University Press,1988.

Catholics for a Free Choice: *Bad Faith at the UN: drawing back the curtain on the Catholic Family and Human Rights Institute,* Washington, DC: Catholics for a Free Choice, 2001.

Gabriel, Marie Cruz: *Children of the street,* New York, Penguin Books, 1994.

Global Policy Forum: *NGOs and the United Nations,* New York, Global Policy Forum, 1999.

Harold K. Jacobson: *Networks of Interdependence: international organizations and the global political system,* New York, Knopf, 1984.

Harry J. Steiner: *Diverse Partners: non-governmental organizations in the human rights movement,* Cambridge, Harvard Law School and Human Rights Internet, 1990.

John Boli and George Thomas: *Constructing World Culture: International Nongovernmental Organizations Since 1875,* Stanford, Stanford University Press, 1999.

John Clayton Thomas: *Public Participation in Public Decision: New Skills and Strategies for Public Managers,* San Francisco, Jossey-Bass Publishers, 1995.

John Ehrenberg: *Civil Society: The Critical History of an Idea,* New York, New York University Press, 1998.

John Foster with Anita Anand: *Whose World is it Anyway? Civil Society, the United Nations and the multilateral future,* Ottawa, United Nations Association of Canada, 1999.

Jonathan A. Fox and L. David Brown: *The Struggle for Accountability: The World Bank, NGOs, and Grassroots Movements,* Cambridge, Mass.: MIT Press, 1998.

Julie Fisher: *The Road from Rio: sustainable development and the nongovernmental movement in the Third World,* Westport, Praeger, 1993.

Marcos Arruda: *NGOs and the World Bank: Is It Possible to Collaborate Critically?,* Rio de Janeiro: PACS, 1995.

Mary Anderson: *Managing Global Chaos: Sources of and Responses to International Conflict,* Washington, DC: United States Institute of Peace Press, 1996.

Paul J. Nelson: *The World Bank and NGOs: The Limits of Apolitical Development,* New York, St. Martin's Press, 1995.

Paul Wapner: *Environmental Activism and World Civic Politics,* Albany, SUNY Press, 1996.

Peter Willetts: *Pressure Groups in the Global System,* London, Francis Pinter, 1982

Thomas Carroll: *Intermediary NGOs: the supporting link in grassroots development,* West Hartford, CT: Kumarian Press, 1992.

Thomas G. Weiss & Leon Gordenker: *NGOs, the UN & Global Governance,* Boulder, Lynne Riener, 1996.

Thomas Princen and Matthias Finger: *Environmental NGOs in World Politics,* London, Routledge, 1994.

Yolanda N. Kakabadse and Sarah Burns: *Movers and Shapers: NGOs in International Affairs,* Washington DC, World Resources Institute, 1994.

Index

□□□